The Keys

D1124800

To Success:

Unlocking College Achievement

Drew Case, RN, MSN

Disclaimer and Terms of Use:

The Author and Publisher has strived to be as accurate and complete as possible in the creation of this book, notwithstanding the fact that he does not warrant or represent at any time that the contents within are accurate due to the rapidly changing nature of the Internet. While all attempts have been made to verify information provided in this publication, the Author and Publisher assume no responsibility for errors, omissions, or contrary interpretation of the subject matter herein. Any perceived slights of specific persons, peoples, or organizations are unintentional.

Printed in the United States of America

First Printing, 2014

ISBN-13: 978-1500386948

ISBN-10: 1500386944

Library of Congress Control Number: 2014915199

CreateSpace Independent Publishing Platform, North Charleston, SC

ACKNOWLEDGMENTS

This book is dedicated to my son Wyatt and my daughter Adree in the hope that someday it will help them to succeed in their pursuit of an education. My hope is that they will find the same passion as I have for learning. I also want to extend a special thanks to my wife Sheena for supporting my dream of seeing this book published. It could not have happened without them. My family is my  inspiration and motivation and everything is possible through them.

I want to thank the thousands of students whose positive feedback helped me create and refine this guide. They inspired me to share my ideas with a wider audience. My hope is that everyone reading these suggestions will find something useful and that they will enjoy reading this book as much as I have enjoyed writing it.

AUTHOR BIOGRAPHY

Drew Case earned both his bachelor of science in nursing and his master of science in nursing from the University of Nebraska Medical Center. He is a registered nurse and was formerly a Lieutenant in the United States Navy Reserve and Acute Adult Nurse Practitioner. He is currently the Executive Director of Southeast Nebraska AHEC and teaches leadership and science classes at Doane College. He reviews textbooks, lab manuals, and exam questions for Elsevier and Pearson.

Case authored *Essentials of Anatomy and Physiology Study Guide* and *Essentials of Anatomy and Physiology: Workbook and Study Guide*, as well as his latest publication, *The Keys to Success*.

Case earned recognition for his work in multiple fields, including a letter of appreciation from the United States Navy Reserve for exceptional achievement, and the Image in Nursing Award from the Bryan Student Nurses Association for exemplifying outstanding leadership.

Case travels presenting to various K-12 schools and colleges. Case is available for speaking and presentations. Please contact him at drew.case@doane.edu for more information.

Contents

THE **KEYS** TO **SUCCESS:**

UNLOCKING COLLEGE ACHIEVEMENT

*"Many receive advice,
only the wise profit by it" – Syrus*

Foreword

Fifteen years ago while I was teaching nursing students, some of my students would come to my office asking how they could do better in school. I soon noticed a pattern in their study habits. Even though I repeatedly covered the same basic material with them, they kept coming back for the same study tips and suggestions I had given them before, as if they had forgotten what we had covered. Finally I decided to put in writing all the study advice I had been giving so the students could review this material as often as necessary. This seemed to work quite well, and the feedback I received was very positive. At that point the material consisted of little more than basic study skills, covering three to four pages.

Many years later, I returned to my true passion of teaching science courses: anatomy, physiology, pathophysiology, and pharmacology. The nursing students I previously taught had passed their science prerequisites, indicating that they acquired some basic understanding of how to study and take exams. After I began teaching prerequisite science courses, I discovered that many, if not the majority, of my students lacked the basic skills required for successful studying and test taking. As a result, I began to update and modify the materials I originally created for my nursing students so I could share them with my science students.

Rather than waiting for students to come to me with concerns about their grades or questions about how to study, I added this material to the syllabus of every class I taught. The response from the students was amazing. Their consistent and positive feedback prompted me to look for ways to improve and supplement my study skills document. It was at this point that I realized studying and performing well in school is an "Art," not so different from many other forms of art. Most of us are not that proficient in the beginning. It takes practice and repetition and, for many, techniques need to be adapted to meet individual needs.

"The roots of education are bitter, but the fruit is sweet" – Aristotle

Over the years I have had many of my students tell me they shared "The Keys to Success" with students in other classes.

3

Interestingly, I found that students not taking my course were buying my syllabus and notes from the college bookstore to help them study.

The purpose of this book is to make the lessons I learned in more than fifteen years of teaching and advising students how to be successful in college accessible to everyone interested in improving their ability to acquire and apply new skills. These concepts can be applied to any situation where material needs to be memorized or a new task needs to be mastered. College is not the only platform for this material. These concepts will work for K–12 education, learning new job skills, and even in the military, as I found when I applied them in my officer training in the United States Navy. The possibilities for the application of these suggestions to anything related to education and learning are endless.

"The way to get to the top is to get off your bottom" – Dr. Eugene Swearingen

HOW TO BE A
SUCCESSFUL
STUDENT

"The future belongs to those who believe in the beauty of their dreams" – Eleanor Roosevelt

If you are still in high school or have just graduated, you are about to become responsible for the course of your life. Overnight you will go from sitting in the passenger seat to driving the car. Decisions you make over the next few years will set the stage for the rest of your life.

Perhaps you are returning to school after many years spent raising a family, serving in the military, or maybe you just want to learn new skills. Although you will bring different experiences and degrees of maturity to the table, the challenge facing you is no different than that confronting young folks right out of high school. In either case, the suggested approach is the same.

The fact that you are reading this book shows you are considering college, are already taking college courses and looking for help, or that you need to learn new skills. You are off to a good start! Unfortunately, success requires a lot more than simply "wanting it." Only you can ***earn*** an education. It will take work and will not be easy. Many of you played sports, and those that did not can still relate to this. Would you ever go to a game or competition without practicing and having a game plan? Of course not! That would be silly and most likely result in failure. Many young people today begin college thinking it's just a continuation of high school, only to discover it's a whole new game and they don't have a "game plan." Don't worry; with some direction and planning, you can have a game plan and be ready to move up to the major leagues.

"Success is never final; failure is never fatal; it is courage that counts" – Winston Churchill

Regardless of why you are reading this material, your goal is the same: ***to be successful!*** Being successful in class or life is not just the result of chance. Achieving an *A* or failing a course is not the result of luck. There are many factors involved in both failure and success. The million-dollar question is ***"What factors lead to success?"*** After teaching for many years, I have noticed a pattern in students who succeed and in those who fail. The interesting thing is that most of you already know what factors lead to success; you just need a way to be reminded of what they are. The following checklist describes steps that will consistently lead students to success. Failure is the result of not doing or understanding these concepts.

"The wise does at once what the fool does at last"

KEY QUESTIONS

There are several important questions you need to ask yourself and be completely honest in your answers. How you answer will be a good indicator of your readiness for college, or if you even want to go to college. Not to sound like a cliché but what do you want to do with your life? Considering this question before starting school is far more important than you might think. That is not to say that you must know exactly what career you want to pursue before starting college. Statistics show us that most students entering college don't have a specific career in mind, and actually discover the answer during college. However, trying to answer this question can help guide you towards what you may want to do, or more importantly, what you don't want to do.

An example of what I am talking about is consideration of becoming a physician. Lots of young people think they would like to be medical doctors, as did I. The money is great and "Wow, I would be a doctor!" What many do not think about is the sacrifices required to become a doctor. If your first priority is to have a family and you want to be a neurosurgeon, you are almost certainly going to be seriously conflicted. You may also like to start your family before the age of thirty. Again, you are likely to run into conflict with incompatible goals.

"Life is a coin. You can spend it any way you wish, but you can spend it only once" – Lillian Dickson

Perhaps your life's dream is to live in the country, but you are interested in a career that is only available in an urban setting. Are you going to be willing to commute daily to work? Over the years I have seen too many students earn degrees in subjects that they were very interested in who are now working at McDonald's as managers. Think very carefully about what you will do with your degree and what jobs will be available with that degree.

If one of your life's goals is to travel the world and go on annual vacations to faraway places and the career you have chosen only starts at $20,000 a year, you are going to have a conflict of interest.

This leads to the question "What is your purpose in life?" Many people do not know what their purpose is and for those that do, it can change. For example, when I was entering college my purpose was to make lots of money. My thought was that I would need lots of money to get what I wanted out of life. As soon as I had children, I realized this was no longer my purpose. Now my purpose was to earn a good living, but my number one focus was spending quality time with my family. These two purposes frequently do not go well together. Do you see where I am going with this? If you are able to identify your purpose, it gives you direction, and direction helps you focus, especially in school. Try to identify your purpose. Write some ideas down and look at them to help you discover your current purpose. Discovering our purpose leads to clarity of mind and significantly increases our chances of success!

"The starting point of all achievement is desire" – Napoleon Hill

Once you discover your purpose, you need to ask yourself "what am I willing to sacrifice in order to achieve my purpose?" Nothing worthwhile comes without sacrifice. To earn your medical degree will require the investment of a significant amount of money and, more importantly, time. This time is usually in your youth and many are not willing to spend most of their twenties in school. "Sacrifice little, achieve little." There is a reason that not everyone makes six-figure incomes. Many of us are not willing to make the sacrifice to earn the degree that leads to such a job. Make sure you know what you are willing to sacrifice before pursuing an education and career.

If you just read the above and are thinking, "Oh my, I really am behind; I have no idea what I want to do, or where I want to go, etc." This is why colleges have career counselors. Make an appointment with one and start doing a little research of your own. There are all kinds of online and free assessments that can help you determine and/or suggest careers you might be interested in. Start with your college career counselor, that's what they are there for. Keep one thing in mind when looking at career options: what you love to do is not always the best career choice. There is a saying "The quickest way to ruin a hobby is to make it a job." I know many people who made their favorite hobby their job and found that it is no longer their hobby or favorite thing to do. Don't get me wrong, I very much believe that you should love what you do for a living even if it is different than what you love to do with your free time or hobbies.

On the first day of class you need to ask yourself some very important questions (actually write out your answers in the space provided; it will help you see any future areas of conflict):

❑ What grade do I want or need?

❑ What grade am I willing to earn? (#1 and #2 should match)

❑ How much time am I willing to spend to earn the grade I want? (hours per day or hours per week)

❑ How much time *can* I spend? (hours per day or hours per week)

❑ What am I willing to do to pass this class? (Spend less time with family, friends, and hobbies, work fewer hours, change schedule, etc.)

❑ What is my ultimate goal?

"Conquer yourself rather than the world" – Descartes

KEY CONCEPTS

First and foremost is understanding that success and failure depend on **you**! Instructors **do not** fail students, students fail students. Instructors simply record what the student has earned. An A+ is earned just the same as an F. It is **imperative** that you believe and understand this concept. This is the single most important key to success. If you do not grasp, buy, believe, and understand this concept, the rest of this book will be of little help. It's up to you—all you!

This concept is called accountability and responsibility. Most of you are very familiar with these terms but let's define them anyway.

Responsibility – being the person who caused something to happen

Accountability – willingness to accept responsibility for one's actions

As the result of many years of teaching many different subjects at colleges, universities, and in the military, I have identified one common characteristic that directly relates to students' success and failure: accepting responsibility and accountability for their achievements or the lack thereof. This does not mean that being responsible and accountable will lead to success, but not being responsible and accountable will almost certainly lead to failure!

"Adversity causes some men to break; others to break records" – William A. Ward

How would an A+ or 4.0 student respond if the instructor claimed that they had been "given" their grade? Would they say, "I don't think so, I earned that grade"? We all know this to be true; 4.0 students sacrifice a lot to maintain that grade. So why is it all so common that when students fail the response is "They were too hard, they failed me." Do you see what I am saying? Whether you want to admit it or not you know what I am saying is true. ***Your success or failure is totally dependent on you***! If you don't believe this, you are going to struggle in college and life.

BE PREPARED

"Luck is a matter of preparation meeting opportunity" – Oprah Winfrey

After accepting the realities of responsibility and accountability, being prepared is probably the next most important concept to grasp. Many of you like football or some other sport. Would any team or individual go to a game, not be prepared, and expect to be successful? No way! So why did so many of my students come to class with no idea of what material we were discussing that day, and then scratch their heads when they failed the course? One reason is because many students have a false perception of what being "prepared" means. We will get into how to study later but being prepared for class does not need to take much time. It mostly involves reviewing what is to be covered, making sure all assignments are done and making sure ***you*** are prepared. Being prepared means arriving to class on time, getting the seat you want or need, getting a good night's sleep (not working the night shift before class), and having a game plan.

"Before anything else, preparation is the key to success" – Alexander Graham Bell

Being prepared also includes choosing the professor that is right for you. When you sign up for a class, you are choosing your instructor, so be sure to make an informed choice. Find out what their teaching style is like. You might even ask to meet them and ask a few questions. Get a feel for their personality and ask them to describe their teaching style and philosophy. What is the worst that could happen? That they refuse to take the time to talk to you? If that happens they may have just answered your questions. I highly recommend taking this step with any subject you feel may be difficult for you. Although you are ultimately responsible, having the right instructor may just make enough difference between success and failure.

"I've always considered myself to be just average talent and what I have is a ridiculous insane obsessiveness for practice and preparation" – Will Smith

If you are returning to school after many years and now have a family and a full time job, being prepared means you have thought out in advance when and where you will be able to study. Do not wait until the class starts to realize you are in way over your head. Find out how much time (hours per week) will be required to be successful in this course.

IT'S A FULL TIME JOB!

A very simple yet effective approach to school is to think of getting an education as your full time job. This attitude will put you in the right mind frame for success. I have discussed this concept throughout the book, but it's so simple and important I wanted to put it all by itself. When you are a student what is one of the most important things in your life? Being successful in school, of course. Once you graduate and get the job of your dreams, then your priority becomes your career or family or both. Let's talk about this dream job. Would you miss work and fail to call in before you were expected to be there? Would you sleep at your desk or on the job? If you are in a meeting with your supervisor, would you text on your phone? If your boss tells you what they need and expect of you, would you argue with them if you disagree? Would you consistently show up late to your dream job? Would you come to work unprepared to do a presentation? Would you come to work consistently tired and sluggish because you were up late the night before partying? Would you come to work hung-over? I think you get the idea by now so one last question.......What would happen if you answered yes to one or more of these questions? That's right, you would get fired, canned, booted, terminated. Think of school for what it is: a full time job that is going to prepare you for the career or job of your dreams. *It's a means to an end!* Treat it as such and you are off to a very good start, trust me.

ONLINE OR IN CLASS?

Online education is a growing trend for colleges and universities. Does this mean it is a better alternative than a traditional classroom for you? Online education was originally designed for distance learning students who lived so far from campus that attending class in person was not an option. Later it became apparent that this method of education also worked well for non-traditional students who worked full time and/or had schedules that made taking a class with set times and dates difficult or impossible. Online courses were a miracle for these folks, and suddenly an education was possible. However the purpose of online education was to supplement, not replace, in class courses. Unfortunately many on campus students or young students living near the school are enrolling in online courses simply to avoid attending a class. Some students view online courses as much easier because of their flexible schedule and the difficulty level of the class. As a result many non-traditional students and others that truly need an online course have great difficulty enrolling in them because they are the first to fill.

Colleges see this as a good thing and the "wave of the future" and thus more and more schools are increasing the number of available online courses. It saves the colleges a tremendous amount of money while making it possible to offer more classes and making more money. If you are the type of student online courses were intended to serve, then what I am going to say is not going to help you in making a decision. However, for all you that can make it to class but are considering the online alternative as a "better" option, **KEEP READING!**

Let's start with asking this – why are you in school? I know what you are thinking: many of you may want to complete your education as quickly and painlessly as possible. Believe me, I hear you and I understand this. However, as an instructor I want your answer to be "to learn." What if we can do both? In my opinion you will learn more in class than online assuming that we (your instructors) are doing our jobs. If we are, class is fun, interesting, relatively painless, and you have the opportunity to achieve a much deeper level of understanding than you ever would online. That is why you want to do a little research on who is teaching the class. If the choice is an instructor that has a reputation for putting all their students to sleep by reading PowerPoint's to them every lecture, take the course online. If the college does not hire quality instructors online may be the better option. This is why you **always, always, always** fill out evaluations on your instructors! If none are offered, ask for them. If none are provided, complain and ask for them. Evaluations should always be done for every class. If you do your homework and find a **good instructor**, you are going to thank me. Nothing can replace sitting in person with a quality instructor when it comes to learning.

Online courses are going to require a lot more **motivation, discipline, organization, and a lot of study time**. If the online course is designed correctly and has the same learning expectations as the in class course, you will probably spend much more of your time to earn the same grade. That's right, more time! I hear this all the time from students that are taking my lecture because they failed the online version of the course. I constantly hear from them "I really wish I had just taken your class from the beginning, I was not learning anything from the online course, and it took way more time." If you are a procrastinator and lack motivation or discipline, stay away from online courses like the plague. You need a good instructor to light your fire, help get you motivated, and teach you some skills. You learn far more in class than just the subject matter. Good instructors teach you study skills, how to motivate yourself, discipline, and much more. You will miss out on these extras in online courses and deprive yourself of the very rich and enlightening experience that a good instructor can provide.

Sad but true, a lot of students take online because they are easier and easier to cheat on. I know that some students hire people to take their tests, write their papers, etc. and this is much easier to do with an online class. I know this because I have attended many college meetings trying to figure out how to prevent this from happening. Really, why are you in school if this is you? The thing is, many students will have to take some certification or board exams after graduating from college, and these are proctored tests that you will **not** be able to cheat on. The students I just described never pass their boards and waste a lot of time and money. Don't you want to learn as much as possible to prepare for these kinds of exams? After all, it does not matter if you are a 4.0 student all the way through college if you can't pass boards!

Bottom line: only take online courses if there is no other choice for you!

WHAT CLASSES TO TAKE, WHEN, AND HOW MANY?

Deciding when and how many classes to take is also part of being prepared. I **strongly** suggest to students to be "gentle" on themselves their first term, quarter, or semester in college. Many students will suffer a mild culture shock when starting college. This is not the best time to load up on hours or to take your most difficult or important courses. I always suggest starting with a nice **easy** schedule with classes you will need. Depending on your career plans, I recommend taking the minimum number of credits first term that will keep you on schedule with your expected graduation date. After completing the first set of classes you will know what to expect, have a feel for college, and be ready to dig in. You will have figured out parking and travel issues, conflicts with work and family, time requirements, how to study, etc. Better to allow yourself some room during that first term for a steep learning curve.

I also suggest not taking two or more similar courses in the same term. It is helpful and beneficial to have variety in courses each term. If at all possible, avoid taking multiple science and math courses in one term. I have rarely observed students being successful doing this. An example of a well-balanced schedule for the first term in college is: English 101, Psychology 101, and Biology 101. After the first year, you will have a better grasp of your strengths and weaknesses and should have little problem planning your schedule with the assistance of an advisor. More on this in the upcoming section "The Right Advisor." When you find the right advisor, they will help you create a plan, or as I like to call it, the "college career schedule." Most colleges, majors, and programs will have a list of all the classes you will need to graduate. Keep this list in a file and in a safe place. Use it as a checklist when it is time to schedule and plan what classes to take. It is so simple and easy to use, yet so many students do not do this and then before registration, they have to try to locate this information and determine what they have taken, etc. They recreate the wheel every time they register for a new term. Work with your advisor, create your college class schedule for your entire education, refer to it each time for registration, and cross off the classes as you complete them. It really is that simple!

"I really am scared to take chemistry, when should I take it?" Most students will put off taking their least favorite classes until the very end. This is terrible planning for many reasons. The biggest concern is that if this class poses a serious challenge, and you wait until your last term before getting accepted into a program or graduating, what is going to happen if you fail the course or do not receive the grade you need or want? I cannot tell you how many times I have seen this happen. It can cause lots of serious unforeseen problems. Most scholarships are based on GPA and require fulltime student status, as does health insurance and many funding sources. If "chemistry" is your last class to take and you have to take it over, you may have to take additional classes you don't need or want simply to maintain fulltime student status. This is why I recommend after your first college term, start taking all the classes you "fear" first. Get them out of the way so if you do have problems and would have to retake a class, you will not find yourself in the scenario described above.

One last thing to consider is trying to schedule all your classes in just two or three days each week. Many students do this thinking it will be better for work, studying, fun time, etc., but there is a down side to consider. If you have a full time schedule, you may be in class *all* day on those two days. Initially this sounds great until the student realizes they are tired and burned out halfway through the day. What frequently happens is the last class of the day suffers. If you are a traditional student, school is your full time job, so I recommend you spread those classes out! You will thank me later. Scheduling all your classes in two or three days also means everything is always going to be due on the same days along with exams. Although this may be the only choice for non-traditional students, all I am saying is really put some thought into it before scheduling your classes.

THE COURSE SYLLABUS IS YOUR "BFF"

As an instructor, I am aware that most students do not read the syllabus or consider it critical to their success. They could not be more wrong. The syllabus is the key to understanding your instructor's expectations (see Expectations) and it can tell you things about their teaching style and personality, which may be very beneficial to you.

A good syllabus will contain everything you need to know to be successful in the course. It will have the schedule, important dates, expectations, requirements, grading scale, assignments, directions, etc. Over the years, I have consistently observed that all the successful students had not only read the syllabus, but also had much of it memorized. Most every student who failed had not read the syllabus. After making this observation, I began including syllabus information on the first exam, and noticed a significant change in my students. Of course they were not all successful, however, they were much more aware of my expectations, which improved their grades and their overall attitude. It clearly made a positive difference to have them be familiar with the syllabus, and putting it on the exam was the best way to assure that result. ***READ THE SYLLABUS!!*** I guarantee you will not regret it or find it to be a waste of time.

THE RIGHT ADVISOR

It is *critical* to find an advisor that you are comfortable with. I cannot stress enough the importance of finding a good advisor. What is a good advisor? One you feel comfortable with and who has knowledge in the field you are planning on going into. If you have no idea what you want to do, find one who is helpful, knowledgeable, and makes you feel comfortable. Your advisor does not have to be an official college "advisor" either. Some schools assign you to an advisor, but by no means are you required to stay with them. An advisor only "advises" you, you don't have to seek or even follow their advice. It's about you and your goals so you may need to look and ask around to find the advisor you want.

"Advice is like snow – the softer it falls, the longer it dwells upon, and the deeper it sinks into the mind" – Samuel Taylor Coleridge

If you want to go into the medical field, you should find someone in the medical field to advise you on what classes to take and when to take them. You may not get the best advice if your advisor is an English professor. You should have an English professor advisor if you are an English major. You may have to take responsibility for selecting your advisor. Some colleges have literally thousands of new students every term. They cannot possibly match up every student with the ideal advisor. This happens all the time: students are not paired with the best advisor and with no ill intent, do not get the best advice. As stated before, "your education, your responsibility." The advisors do the best they can with the knowledge they have. Some will tell you "I don't think I am the best advisor for you." Don't take it personally; it's in your best interest!

EMBRACE MISTAKES

"Failure is the key to success; each mistake teaches us something" – Morihei Ueshiba

"A mistake is only a mistake if we do not learn something, so don't make mistakes." You are going to make a lot of mistakes in school, so embrace them, learn from them, and don't make them again. I have seen too many students melt down the first time they fail an exam, forget an assignment, etc. Expect mistakes, know they will happen, and accept the fact that it is impossible to avoid them.

In fact, the more you fear mistakes, the more likely they become. My young students love this example!

Tom and Sally are a couple in high school. Tom has a bit of a jealously issue. He is worried that Sally is going to fall for some other guy in their school. Tom's behavior is suspicious and becoming increasingly annoying to Sally. This in turn is picked up by Tom who now becomes more insecure and further annoys Sally. Eventually, what does Sally do? That's right, she discovers that Bob is much more enjoyable to spend time with because he is not constantly grilling her about what she is doing and whom she is talking to. Sally dumps Tom on the spot and discovers true love with Bob who is secure and confident and makes Sally feel good about herself.

"Success is how high you bounce when you hit bottom" – George S. Patton

The more we fear something, the more it affects our behavior and can lead to the very thing we fear. The hardest part of making a mistake is admitting it. When you are able to admit to your mistakes you are accepting accountability and responsibility.

Mistakes are inevitable, embrace them! What else can you do?

"FEELING OVERWHELMED, OUT OF CONTROL?" YOU MAY NEED HELP!

Being young is challenging enough, but now you have complete freedom and your life has changed overnight. Most of us that are older often wonder how we made it through our youth. It can be the best time of your life, but it is also the most challenging and frequently the most dramatic. You have not had the years we have had to develop the skills to deal with the drama that life throws at us and to realize that life goes on. The boyfriend that just dumped you was not the man you were going to marry. Failing Chemistry 101 did not end your career dreams. However, when you are young it does not feel that way and you don't know these things because you are living them right now!

Many young people come to college with issues they have been dealing with, often for some time. Many of them have never shared their concerns with their parents and probably have not seen someone (professionally) regarding the issue(s). Now before you say, "This does not apply to me; I don't need to see someone," think about this: if I told you that you have high cholesterol that is genetic and will not come down with diet and exercise, would you try to treat it by yourself or with wishful thinking? What if you have a family history of high cholesterol and heart disease? Would you see a professional and take medication if they thought you needed it? Maybe they discover that it's not genetic and can be treated with diet and exercise. I hope you are following me, if not pay better attention, because this is important.

A large percentage of the US population deals with depression, anxiety, panic attacks, eating disorders, and insomnia, and a large percentage of these people do not seek professional help to figure out how to deal with their condition. Frequently the issues are resolved without medication. All that is needed is some good old "talking about what is the problem" and learning new ways to deal with things. It has never ceased to amaze me that people think they do not need to learn or be to be taught how to deal with life and the problems that life throws at us. They think we just automatically know how to best deal with stress. **REALLY?** You need to be taught how to ride a bike or read a book but you don't have to be taught how to deal with sexual assault, death in the family, physical or emotional abuse, addictions, depression, stress, etc.? I hope I have made my point that there is nothing wrong with admitting that you may benefit from talking to a professional. What do you have to lose?

The nice thing about college is most of them offer professional counseling services for **free!** It's completely confidential which means your parents, future employers, etc. will never know. This may be your chance to work on some issues that have been weighing you down for a long time or impairing your life.

"TO DROP, OR NOT TO DROP" THAT IS THE QUESTION

It is not an enjoyable topic to cover, and I hope you will never have to use this information, but it is always better to have a plan and make an informed decision. It may not even have anything to do with you or your study habits. Students get sick or injured, have a family member die, are deployed by the military, or have a baby. Sometimes life just gets too demanding and we get too far behind to catch up. Bottom line, if you find yourself so deep in the hole for whatever reason, you need to make a decision. If it is due to circumstances completely out of your control, talk to your instructor and the admissions office! Most colleges are very understanding and will work with you. I have seen many students get a refund, get credit for the next time, and not receive a failing grade. This is why you treat school like a job. If your instructor is aware of your situation, they will most likely help you with this process. **Do not** wait until the end and suddenly inform your instructor that you missed the last month of class because you were in a car accident and have been in the hospital (yes, this happened and no, they were not in the intensive care unit or unconscious). They will most likely not be able to do anything at that point. Again, think of school as a job. If I am sick and miss work, I call before my shift, not a week later. I have had parents call me to let me know their child is in the hospital, and it is my pleasure to work with them and help the student as much as possible. I have helped many students through some of the most difficult times in their lives, but it is only because they kept me in the loop and asked for my help.

What if you simply did not study right or plan enough time, and now you are failing? Well, you need to make a decision. You have to ask yourself a **very** important question and you have to be honest with the answer: "Can I get the grade out of this class I want or need with the time I have left?" If the answer is yes, simple: don't drop the class as long as it will not drag other classes down while bringing this one up. Don't forget to include that consideration in your equation when deciding if you can pass the course. If the answer is no, you need to consider dropping it, but there are many things to consider before doing this. Are you passed the drop date to get some money back and keep it off your record? They are usually one in the same. If the answer is no, it's a much simpler choice. I usually recommend to students with this option to drop the class, do better in their other classes, and plan better next time as long as it does not affect something else like financial aid, scholarships, or insurance. If the answer is yes, we continue on with things to consider. Are you on a scholarship that will be more affected by dropping a class or failing a class? With the major or program you are in or considering, is there a limit or negative consequence for dropping a class vs. failing a class? Will dropping the class drop you below full time status and if so, will it affect insurance or other things? If you are not paying for your school I would highly recommend you consult with whoever is!!!

You do not want to bite the hand that feeds you, if you catch my drift. There are a great many things to consider before dropping a class and I would strongly recommend that you speak with someone in the college regarding this before making a decision. I would start with the instructor and also include the admissions office and your advisor.

Bottom line, dropping a class can be a good thing or a bad thing depending on the student and their situation so make sure you have all the facts before making the decision and ***don't*** put this decision off, you may miss an opportunity!

"HOW YOU SHOW UP"

"Be the change you want to see in the world" – Gandhi

I want to sell my older car. The engine is not in the best shape but the car body is in good condition. It has been sitting under a tree in the driveway and is covered with bird poop. Would I sell this car covered in bird poop and expect top dollar? I know it's a silly question but students frequently show up to class, lay their head on the desk and sleep during class, text on their cell phone, and generally present with not the best attitude. Then when they are failing, want me to take my time to help them. Even if they pass the class, they ask me to write them a letter of reference. They are trying to sell me a car covered in bird poop, and are asking top dollar for it. Strange example but it does drive home the basic concept with perfect clarity!

The car does not have the best engine, but if I wash and wax the outside, detail the inside and make it smell good, I may just get much more for it than I expected. We are very visual beings and we do judge a book by its cover! Don't be upset if you have been judge by how you show up. That's life.

"Politeness goes far, yet costs nothing" – Seneca

What I am getting at is **how we show up makes a big difference**. When I show up with **attitude,** it's the same as throwing a great big spotlight on myself for the instructor. "No matter what I do, they are never happy, they are just waiting for me to make a mistake." Students do not like being in the spotlight and neither do I. If you don't want to be in the spotlight or under a microscope, don't show up with a bad attitude. This applies not just to school but **everything** in life.

If you start feeling that your teacher, professor, or supervisor does not like you and is making things difficult for you, perform an attitude reality check. Should you find you have an attitude and are not showing up the way you should, lose the attitude and **get your mind right**. Most of the time when we show up with our mind right, we get removed from the spotlight!

"One important key to success is self-confidence. An important key to self-confidence is preparation" – Arthur Ashe

Sometimes we don't get this figured out until we are **really** under the microscope. At that point it may require some help to change. First, focus on "me" and not "you." Never go to an instructor and start with "you." You just get yourself in deeper. Ask how or what you can do to improve things. Have your instructor help you formulate a **game plan** to get out from the hole you have dug. As instructors, we **love** nothing more than students accepting accountability, and we get all goofy and excited and bend over backwards to help you. This is a team effort, and both parties have the same goal: **success!** To us, that is a far greater lesson learned than what we are actually teaching you, and now you have our attention in a good way.

Do not use the word "fair" when communicating with instructors. It will get you the exact opposite of what you want. Your parents should have told you life is not fair; your instructors are not going to want to explain this concept to you. It is what it is and you most likely put yourself in the situation you are in where you want to use the word fair.

"The best revenge is to be unlike him who performed the injury" – Marcus Aurelius

Show up confident to class and clinical, even if you are unprepared or nervous. Do not draw unnecessary attention to your lack of preparation or fear. Let's look again at the car example. Make it look nice and maybe some minor imperfections or issues might be over looked. If you have ever been to a dog park, it is interesting to watch the animals' behavior. The more fearful and passive a dog is, the more it invites aggression from other dogs. Don't get me wrong, I am not suggesting being dishonest or presenting yourself as more prepared than you are, but we respond more positively to confident people. You are more likely to find yourself under the microscope if you show up nervous, scared, etc. As instructors we associate these behaviors with lack of preparation. There is a saying that relates specifically to this that most of you are familiar with: "Fake it till you make it." Research shows that you can actually "Fake it till you become it." How we show up directly affects our behavior and performance. In other words, simply having confidence can increase your chances of success!

"A strong, positive self-image is the best possible preparation for success" – Joyce Brothers

STRESS MANAGEMENT

"I've failed over and over and over again in my life and that is why I succeed" – Michael Jordan

I just failed Chemistry 101. Twenty years from now what is that going to mean?........... Most likely, nothing! **Keep it in proportion.** This is a really hard concept for young people to grasp. I have also had a lot of adult students that struggle with this to. Even I find myself needing to remember this! When it comes to stress, one the best tools we can employ is to keep the event in proportion. Failing one exam is not the end of the world. Failing the class is usually not the end of a career. The worst thing is usually the loss of the tuition money and a big hit to our ego. Here are a few concepts to keep in mind to help with stress in school:

"Don't sweat the small stuff" – We spend way too much time worrying about the little things in life over which we have absolutely no control. Save your energy for where it is really needed, because our energy is not limitless and you can and will burnout or run out of gas, and this frequently leads to stress and physical illness. Focus on what you can *change* and what really matters. If you can't change the situation or yourself, move on. Remember, because this is extremely important, you can only change yourself. You have no control over others, nor can you change them despite the most valiant efforts. You will simply waste time and energy that could be better used somewhere else.

"Keep it in proportion (in 20 years....)" – Most of you have heard this and know how it goes. The simplest concepts and lessons in life are the most difficult to employ. Think back to some recent events that got you very upset. Now think about how you might feel about them in 20 years. The vast majority of the time we smile and think "yeah, not really a big deal." All that is needed is to remember to stop and do this. It really can be that simple. Next time you get into an argument with friends or family, or are just in an irritating situation, try this and see what happens.

"Be elastic, not spastic"

"God grant me the strength to accept the things I cannot change, courage to change the things I can, and the wisdom to know the difference" – many of you may be familiar with this and associate it with Alcoholics Anonymous but hey, it can't be stated much simpler or better than this!

"Success consists of going from failure to failure without loss of enthusiasm" – Winston Churchill

You must have a balance between work, sleep, family/friends, exercise, playtime, and school. The whole purpose of this book is to make you efficient and effective at studying so you will have time to do other things. College should be one of the best times of your life. You should have a great time, experience new people and events but you also need to get good grades to achieve your life or career goals. Stress will work against you! The more stress free you are, the more effective you are.

One of the best methods of decreasing stress is regular exercise. Use exercise to clear your head between studying. It works and it works great! It is also a fantastic way to decompress after an exam or turning in a difficult assignment. **Manage your stress and help your success.**

Your first credit card is usually received in college. I remember when I started college, the dorm was flooded with credit card offers. Most of them had a low credit limit and did not need your parent's signature. *Be very careful with this!* Some companies will quickly raise your credit limit and frequently charge as much as 21% interest. Many students quickly find themselves in bad way financially before they have even graduated from college. Leave your credit limit low and pay it off every month!!!! **Never let it go to the next month. Never!**

TAKE A BREAK!

Right after Stress Management is the perfect place to put this topic. It may seem odd to suggest that college students should take a break, because many of you reading this might be thinking your problem is not working hard enough, but let's really look at this subject and see what I mean by taking a break and when to take it.

I found it extremely beneficial to reward my good study habits by taking breaks. Assume I have a difficult exam Friday morning and have been studying all week, and have been keeping up in my classes. This weekend I have been invited to go camping at the lake with several friends from college. Use this opportunity to your advantage; use it as a reward for hard work. I know that next week I have nothing due at the beginning of the week and I can afford to take the weekend off after my exam on Friday. I study hard all week, knowing that when I finish the exam on Friday afternoon, I am on a mini-vacation until Monday morning when it's back to business. This accomplishes several things: it is one of the best motivators in the short-term, it reinforces positive behavior, and most of all you get a much needed break before starting all over on Monday. This process should repeat over and over until you complete your education. It may not be every weekend, but you understand my point and it works. Some describe college as a marathon and I strongly disagree with this, as this leads to fatigue and burnout. I think the better approach is a series of sprints with short breaks in between to rest, relax, and catch your breath before the next sprint.

I apply the same principle during the week while studying hard for the exam on Friday. I study hard on-and-off each day (determine in advance how long and what I want to accomplish each session) with a reward at the end of each day. I am a morning person and an introvert, and I like to end each day with some quite time to myself watching a good movie or TV program. I like to rent a movie the night before the exam and watch it as a reward (taking a break) for proper preparation for the exam. If you have prepared as I suggested, you should only be doing some light reviewing the day before the exam anyway. I would have a nice meal and watch a fun movie the night before the exam after my last review for the day. This was very relaxing and I would get a good night sleep. After the exam (usually feeling quite good about how I did), I did something fun that night too if I had nothing that needed immediate attention. In psychology, they call this classic conditioning. You are not so different from Pavlov's dogs, and you simply are conditioning yourself to work hard for a reward. The great thing is this spills over into your everyday life, and I have found it plays a significant role in my success in life. ***Work hard so you can play hard!***

SETTING GOALS

There are entire books out there on setting goals. I don't think you necessarily need to read them unless you are consistently struggling with reaching your goals. Achieving your goals is really quite simple as long as you follow a few basic principles that everyone seems to agree on.

Your goals need to be *specific* and *measurable*. Example: I will read chapters three to six today in my psychology text. This is very specific and measureable. "I will study today" is definitely not specific and questionable if it's measurable.

Not only should you make your goals specific and measurable, you need to make sure that you can reach them or that they are *reachable*. The example above is most likely a very reachable goal. A poorly set goal (specific and measureable but not reachable) is "I will read my entire psychology text today." Students often set unrealistic goals that they cannot possibly achieve. What is *realistic* to one student may not be realistic to another. You have to know yourself and your limits to be able to set realistic goals that are reachable or *achievable*.

The last thing that everyone agrees upon is set a *timetable* for achieving the goal. "I will finish my psychology text two weeks from now by reading a minimum of two chapters a day." A great example that many think of in life is "I want to be rich." Well, this goal lacks just about everything and thus most people never achieve it. Take a little time and think about some goals you have and put them to the test to see what you come up with. Most goals are not achieved without meeting these criteria. I will give you a hint, be **SMART** with your goal setting!

HABITS – THE GOOD, THE BAD, AND THE UGLY!

"**Y**ou are the summation of your habits." If I am a positive and fun person to be around, that is because I am in the habit of looking at things in a positive way. The same holds true for those that are always negative. A+ or 4.0 students are in the habit of getting good grades and that comes from their study habits.

"The direction in which education starts a man will determine his future in life" – Plato

Consider exercise. To get into shape usually is not the most enjoyable process and for many of us can be difficult and even painful at times. It requires sacrifice and time. What happens when we exercise long enough (six months really seems to be the key)? We get into shape and we actually don't feel well if we fail to exercise. It takes much less time to stay in shape than it does to get in shape. It has become a habit and we feel compelled to do it even when we shouldn't. Use this knowledge of habits to your advantage.

We all know that breaking a habit is much harder than starting one, so get into good study habits ASAP if you want to be more successful and have more time to do other things. The key here is to **START STRONG!** You will lose motivation and energy as time goes on, so you want to start as strong as possible to get off on the right foot. You do not want to start this journey from last place and get behind before you even get going, *start strong!* It is much easier to keep the pace in the front rather than try to catch up from the back.

EXPECTATIONS

"If you align expectations with reality, you will never be disappointed" – Terrell Owens

The key to meeting your instructor's expectations is to make sure you know what they are. It sounds like common sense but so does everything else covered to this point. Some instructors are crystal clear about what they expect and you know exactly what needs to be done. However some instructors are not so clear in what they expect and it is up to you to make sure you get the clarity you need to meet their expectations.

This is where you focus on "me" and not "you." Yes, it would be great if the expectations of all of your instructors were crystal clear but this is not always the case. Don't focus on how the instructor should have done something or on what they could do better; instead focus on you and what you need to do if you want to be successful. When faced with this situation you need to know exactly what the expectations of the instructor and the course are. No, it's not fair (remember, never use this word), but you may have to meet with the instructor and ask a lot of questions in order to find out what their specific expectations are. Some instructors may not even be clear on what they expect, and this will be difficult. **You** are the one who needs the clarity, not them. A good instructor realizes this and will make every attempt to set clear and realistic expectations but let's face it, not all instructors will be good. **Your** grade, **your** success, and **your** responsibility.

You cannot meet expectations if you don't know what they are so make sure you understand exactly what is expected of you.

What about your expectations? They are just as important as your instructor's. I don't mean your expectations of your instructor or the college; I mean your expectations of yourself. You need to have clear and above all else, *realistic* expectations for yourself. When I refer to expectations, I often am referring to goals too. You need to know what your expectations are so you can meet them. This is why it is so important to make them realistic. "Why would I make unrealistic expectations for myself?" Students do it all the time. A perfect example is a typical 21 year-old student who is taking a full class load, works a part time job, has a significant other, is on an athletic scholarship, and is struggling to keep a 4.0 GPA. I am not saying it is impossible to accomplish all of this at the same time because many students do, but I do not feel that the student has very realistic expectations without experiencing stress, anxiety, and more.

I am absolutely terrible at English. My English professor in college told me so, but this was not news to me. We became close friends and he became one of my mentors in college. It was unrealistic for me to expect I could get an A+ in his course. He later told me, with a smile, that he had doubts I would pass. I struggled in that subject as long as I could remember but I had realistic expectations of myself and was not disappointed in the least when I received a C+ in English 101.

Each of us is different, so each of us will have different realistic expectations for the same situation. Another example is a student returning to school after a 10-year career that has a full time job with a family and is expecting to take a full time class schedule. In my experience, depending on the student, I would say this is a very unrealistic expectation.

"How much time am I expected to study for this class?" A very common question and a very important one. The rule of thumb is 2:1, or two hours out of class for every hour in class. That means that if the class meets six hours a week you should be spending an additional 12 hours *per week* studying for this class. I always loved pointing this out the first day of class and watching the expressions on my students' faces. Their eyes got big, mouths opened, and some got a little pale. Relax! This is a "rule of thumb." That means if you have no idea what this class is going to be like, but want some idea to plan your school, work, and family schedules, use the 2:1 ratio. Yes, some of your classes will require this much, but others will not. Let's just say I love science and I took human anatomy in high school and did well. Am I going to need 12 hours a week outside of class to get a good grade in my college anatomy class? Most likely not. I never took physics in high school and I don't like science, will I spend 12 hours out of class for six hours in class? Probably not, you will spend more!

HINT: *If you use the 2:1 rule you are usually good-to-go for scheduling work, family, and classes because most students **on average** do it in less time. **Always over estimate your needs and be***

pleasantly surprised, rather than under estimate them and do
poorly or, even worse, fail the class and have to take it again.
Now how much time will you have lost?

KEY TO REFERENCES

You will need references for most careers. For most new graduates those references will need to come from former instructors. It is a good idea to remember this when you are attending classes. If you frequently show up with attitude to class, you may find it very difficult to get a good reference, or any reference at all. What are you saying to the instructor when you lay your head on the desk other than during breaks? What are you saying when you play with your phone during class? What are you saying when you sit with your head hitting the back of the chair? What are you saying when you have a disgusted look on your face during class?

"What you do speaks so loud that I cannot hear what you say" – Ralph Waldo Emerson

Pay attention to your body language, because you are speaking during class without ever saying a word, and you are being judged by your language. Is that fair? You bet – we all do it every day! We are wired to read body language. Sometimes, it can even be more reliable than verbal communication.

When you ask an instructor for a reference, be very clear on what kind of reference you want. You do not want an "ok" or "good" reference, you want a **great, outstanding, excellent** reference, and that is what you need to ask for.

People generally do not like conflict and most of us especially do not like to make people feel bad. If you just ask: "Can I use you as a reference?" it is easy to say "sure" even though if you asked, "Would you give me an outstanding reference?" the answer would be "no."

A majority of the time, people will not lie to you, but they may not go out of their way to tell you that they can only give you an "ok" or "good" reference. If you are applying to a highly competitive school, program, or job, you need the best reference you can get. Trust me, you can see in your instructor's eyes how excited they are to give you a reference. You only want the best, so be very specific about what kind of reference you want. I tell students exactly what kind of reference I will give them and always offer to let them read it first before deciding if they want to use it. I would suggest you ask for this opportunity. If the instructor is not comfortable letting you do this, it suggests they may be uncomfortable with allowing you to read what they have to say about you. If that is the case you do not want to use them as a reference. Think about it, why would someone not want you to read what they have to say about you? *A reference can make or break you!*

One more thing to think about when interacting with your instructors: many of them are well connected in the career paths in which they are teaching. For example, I taught nursing for many years and now most of my former students are experienced and valued members of staff in healthcare facilities all over the state. Many are in administrative and management positions and are charge of hiring new graduates. My reference carries a lot of weight with them, and I have even been able to assist in locating jobs for some of my better students.

I had surgery many years ago, and every single individual in the operating room (other than the surgeon) was a former student of mine. That included the anesthetist, nurses, surgical techs, radiology techs, and even the aide that took me back to my room. How comfortable would you be in that situation? I have always taught my classes with this scenario in mind, and it was actually quite comforting. They were all great students and we were making jokes "Drew, do you remember that bad test grade you gave me?" and laughing right up until I went to sleep. I knew I was in good hands! The point of the story is many of your instructors are **very well** connected and can be an incredible asset to have. Keep in their good graces when possible; they may just help you find a job after college.

STILL IN HIGH SCHOOL?

If you are still in high school as you read this, you are really fortunate. You still have time to make necessary changes before it is too late. What I mean by this is very soon your education is going to cost you a lot of time and someone a lot of money. If you are not successful, that time and money will be wasted. College transcripts will follow you the rest of your life. You will need them for your job. Sadly, no one is interested in how you did in high school after you have attended college. They will be focused on what you did in college. High school grades are important for getting into the school you want and getting scholarships. The purpose of high school is to get you ready for college. The purpose of college is to prepare you for a career and life.

"Education is not preparation for life; education is life itself" – John Dewey

If you think "Oh, so I really don't need to get good grades in high school or even worry about my grades," you really need to go back and re-read the section on habits! I can tell almost every time which of my students earned good grades in high school without ever seeing them. In fact, I can usually tell simply by how they show up and by their body language. High school is your chance to establish good habits before your education costs money and the outcome is more important. It is your opportunity to practice "how you show up" for school.

Use the time you have left in high school to get ready for college. What is more important than the grades you are earning is what you are doing and learning about how to get those grades. Take this time to learn how to study. It is far better to try new and different ways of learning and studying now rather than waiting until you are in college when your education is costing money. Now is the time to experiment with your learning, or the "trial and error" approach.

"I would rather fail in the cause that someday will triumph than triumph in a cause that someday will fail" – Woodrow Wilson

Now is also your opportunity to take as many courses as you can for **FREE**! If you have even a thought about going into a science related field or the medical field, take every science course you can **NOW**. You do not want to experience chemistry or physics for the first time in college. **Trust me**, you will be very sorry. I was.

When I present to high school students getting ready to graduate, I like to ask them some questions:

*"You graduate soon, right?....(they all get a big smile)...what is going to happen when you go off to school?......(the smile gets really big)...are you going to move out of your parent's house?...(then everyone speaks with a loud **YES**)...Oh, what does that mean?...(they look confused, not sure what I am asking)....When will you go to bed? What will you eat? When will you eat? When will you study?....(at this point they are all answering with "**whenever I want**" and the smiles are from ear to ear)...None of you are looking forward to this, are you?....(then everyone begins laughing and speaking)"*

What I am getting at is you are going to be **FREE** for the first time in your life. You may find it difficult to concentrate on school. If your goal is to be a medical professional, you have never taken chemistry before, and now you are taking it in college at 8:00 a.m., you will wish you had some idea what your instructor is talking about. You will wish you could go back in time and take chemistry in high school when life was not so complex and your education was free. Get as much education as you can now so you have more time to enjoy that new freedom in college *and* keep your grades up as well.

Most people that attended college would say they would have done some things differently in high school knowing what they know now. I never took chemistry or physics in high school and was required to take both courses in college. They were not fun. They took a **HUGE** amount of my time compared to human anatomy and physiology, biology, and zoology, which I did take in high school. In fact anatomy was so easy and enjoyable in college that I got a job teaching anatomy labs and got paid great money while in school! That sure beat working in a restaurant (did that too). How cool was that to be 21 and teaching human anatomy labs at the university?

The only reason this opportunity was even possible was because I did so well in the class. It is unlikely that I would have done that well had I not taken the course in high school.

"Man cannot discover new oceans unless he has the courage to lose sight of the shore" – unknown

START THINKING ABOUT COLLEGE BEFORE YOU GET THERE!

You really need to start thinking about college during your first or second year of high school, and perhaps much sooner depending on what college you want to attend. Much of this will also apply if you are returning to school as an adult learner. Start by asking yourself where you want to go, where you can afford to go, and where you can get accepted. All three answers really need to be the same or you have a problem!

Really think about where you want to go to college. I know young people think they can't wait to get far away from home, and there is nothing wrong with that, but there is a lot to consider. Returning adults are more frequently concerned with cost and time issues. In either case, the most important thing to consider is does the school offer what *you* want for an education and does it fit best with your career choice?

If you know where you want to go, make sure you know what the college's admission requirements are well in advance so you will have time to take all of the necessary courses before applying.

If you are interested in biology but the school you would like to attend does not have the *best* biology program, you need to consider what career you are looking at. Sometimes where you received your degree makes no difference, but other times it does. This would be good to know before spending a lot of time and money attending the wrong school for you. If the jobs you will be applying for don't care whether you received your degree from Harvard or the local community college, you will want to seriously consider the cost of your education compared to what you can earn. If you want a highly competitive job in a very specialized field (neurosurgeon), do you want to get your degree or even your prerequisites at the local community college? You may want to look into this before starting a college. One is no better than the other unless cost is an issue or it makes a difference to the program/career you want to get into. The answers to these questions best come from people in the careers you are considering rather than the colleges you are looking at. How it **should be** and how it **really is** are not always the same.

Who is paying for your college education and how much does it cost? Why is the national average student loan debt extremely high? Students did not think about cost before getting their education. You can usually borrow more than you actually need to pay your tuition. Based on the national average amount of student loan debt, it would appear that many students borrow all that is available. Why? When you are young and looking at starting a career that will pay you more money than you have ever seen, you think: "Oh, I can pay that loan off in no time. I will be making hordes of money." The problem is you have not thought about the new car you will want after getting that new job, or the house you will want to park that new car in front of, or the family that you will put in that new house and car. The less you owe when you graduate, the more you will have to spend on fun or necessary things for you and your family.

Money should never be a reason for **NOT** going to college. There are many options for financial assistance. With many opportunities for scholarships, grants, loans, work study, etc. no student should say, "I can't afford to go to college." If all else fails, you can get training in the military or use funds earned in the military. There is also the G.I. bill or other similar opportunities provided by the military. Some employers offer tuition forgiveness or will pay off your student loans in return for your agreement to work for them. There are so many opportunities that few people can honestly say they could not afford to go to college if they really want to. Any college's office of admissions would be more than happy to show you how you can afford to go to their school if possible. If there is a way, they will find it for you. Their job is to make it possible for you to attend their school. Use their knowledge and resources to your advantage. Again, *never ever* let the words come forth from your mouth "I could not afford to go to college" because we both know the truth. Where there is a will, there *is* a way!

"An investment in knowledge pays the best interest" – Benjamin Franklin

Never think a college is out of your price range or is unaffordable until you have actually met with an admission counselor and discussed *your* cost and opportunities. I have heard many students say, "Oh, I would love to go to that school, but I can't afford it" and they have never talked with the school about financial aid. They just know it is a private and/or expensive school. What they don't know is that particular school has financial aid opportunities available that would make it no more expensive than the local state college or university. If you want to go somewhere, *never assume* the school is too expensive for you until you check it out!

NON-TRADITIONAL STUDENTS

Non-traditional students will experience school very differently than those students entering college right out of high school. As a non-traditional student you are bringing an entirely different set of skills and level of experience with you. Many of you are married, or have been, and have a family and a career or are looking to change careers. You can benefit from almost everything in this book, but this section is just for you.

The biggest challenge for the non-traditional student is simply being a student again, and being surrounded by young people. For most of you in this situation, it has been a long time since someone has told you what to do, how to do it, and when to do it. This may not be as easy as you think to deal with. "I am not a young kid, why are you treating me like this?" Don't forget that most of your peers are young kids right out of high school who need guidance and structure. Instructors can't make different rules for different students, and it will be difficult at times for you to deal with class rules and policies given your age and experience. Unfortunately, it has to be that way, but it can be a bit painful for the adult ego sometimes. I would not say I run into this a lot but it's not uncommon to see this be a source of stress for non-traditional students, especially when they make a simple mistake and lose points off an assignment. Just remember, you are in the big melting pot with all the other students and you have to follow the same rules that they need.

Many of you may even be much older than your instructors. We don't like to admit it, but it can be difficult sometimes to be told what to do, when to do it, and how to do it by someone much younger and less experienced than ourselves. Don't think of your instructor in this way; that's the key. They are the expert in what they are teaching and they have what you want, a degree! It's nothing but ego causing you this difficulty. Don't let your ego get in the way of your learning! Most of the time (99%) I love my non-traditional students because they love to learn. Be flexible and keep an open mind and you will do just fine.

THE TECHNOLOGY DEBATE?

Technology is found in more and more of our classrooms every day. Like anything, it can be very useful and assist with your learning, but it can also be misused and interfere with your learning. It's not just the younger generation that has embraced the technology craze, it's everyone. I have been told that I am a dinosaur and I need to get with the times. Don't misunderstand me, I think technology has its place in the modern classroom but just because something is old does not mean it is no longer effective any more than something being new means it's the best. I love technology as much as the next person but I don't think it's the one answer to replace everything when it comes to learning. Let's talk about some specifics and you decide for yourself.

Some would say in this day and age that the physical textbook is on its way out. Maybe so, but it still offers some advantages that you may want to consider. If you drop it, it will not break. It will not run out of power. It can't get a virus. It's easy to loan to friends. And for many people, there is just something about having something tangible in their hands that they can write on and take notes in. Looking at computer monitors can be more strenuous on the eyes, and there are studies concluding that viewing computer monitors before going to bed interferes with sleep patterns. Bottom line, if you like the computer version of books much better, then it's an easy decision because it's about what works best for you. I do find it interesting that even though colleges and publishers are trying to move more to online books, etc., every time I ask my students, the **vast majority** of them say they prefer the good old fashion text book. Makes you wonder who really thinks it's the best idea and why? Could it be because they make more money with online books? I will say that they can be much more convenient and you can read them on your phone or tablet, but this does not mean it's the **best**. Simply ask yourself a very important question: which will you learn better from?

I don't recommend bringing your computer to class for the purpose of taking notes. I think this can work well for some but for most, especially the younger students, the temptations are too great to get distracted, if you know what I mean. This may change someday but for now I have not seen it work very well, and my recommendation would be to continue with paper and pen.

Where technology really excels is in all the resources that are now available instantly at your fingertips. We can look up anything during class in seconds. There are many free opportunities to practice taking quizzes and exams. In human anatomy, for example, you can find dozens of free sites that have actual human cadavers and models where you can quiz and test yourself using the same models you see in your lab. This is an incredible resource and an appropriate use of technology. Almost every phone today has a camera included that can take incredible pictures. My anatomy students took pictures of the models and charts we were using so they could review them at home. What a great idea! When I was a student, this was not an option. If you wanted to look at the models, you had to come to open lab on Friday. What if you worked? Now you can take the models home with you. You could even do study groups via the computer with cameras and things like FaceTime or Skype. Now you can study with classmates that don't even live in the same town as you without the long drive. These are just a few examples of how technology can greatly enhance your learning. Technology, like so many other things, can be good or bad depending on how it is used.

UNDERSTANDING SUCCESS

Many people like to believe that success is something that only comes to a few or is related to luck. This could not be further from the truth. Success is really quite simple. It's a choice and it's your choice. The key to understanding how to succeed is to accept that success or failure is the result of your choices. Everything I have said thus far is to help you learn that you need to understand, believe, accept and begin to practice this principal. Everything following is to give you different choices to make, and try to help you be successful. Being successful may not be easy because it takes sacrifice and hard work, but understanding how to achieve success is easy.

THE ART OF STUDYING

"The secret of success is to do the common things uncommonly well" – John D. Rockefeller, Jr.

There is an art to studying. Anyone one can **study**, but few truly learn the art. The more you practice, the better you get, and what could be more important than truly being good at studying? The better you are at studying, the more time you have to play and enjoy life. Let's be honest, college is about finding and preparing for a career but it is also about having fun. You are only going to be young once, so you should have fun and enjoy the best college experience possible with memories that last a lifetime. If you are coming back to school later in life this may not be appealing to you, or even possible with job, family, etc. Either way, the better and more efficiently you study, the more time you have to do what you want or need to do. In addition, you get better grades, reach your career goals, and become more successful. The sooner you start practicing, the sooner you can begin to enjoy the benefits of *The Art of Studying*.

Use the following as a *checklist*. If you find you are having difficulty in a class, go through this list and *check off* the steps you are doing. Often students will find that they don't have much checked and the reason is pretty obvious. If you have many or most of the steps checked, re-read them to see if you are missing something simple yet critical. Many times the simplest things are the most important ones. This process is one of trial and error. If you still can't find things to improve on in how you study, seriously consider how you are taking exams, review that section, and look for areas to improve upon. Let's get started!

❑ BE ON TIME TO CLASS

If you are one of those people who are consistently late, plan on being in class fifteen minutes early (to give yourself a buffer). Students who are consistently late rarely pass. It's not so much that they are missing valuable information in those one or two minutes, but they have the wrong attitude, and *attitude is everything* when it comes to success! An instructor can almost predict failure based solely on this factor.

Important announcements, vital changes, and information are most frequently given right at the beginning of class. If you are late, be sure to ask a fellow student what you missed. It is usually better to ask a fellow student what you missed rather than asking the instructor, especially if you have been late to class before. Consider the impression you are making if you keep asking your instructor to fill you in on what you missed from being late to class. You are only going to make matters worse by asking them to take time to fill you in for what you missed due to your tardiness. If being late is a one-time thing and you have been an outstanding student and something unexpected comes up, by all means ask your instructor for help. They usually are more than happy to accommodate you in those situations.

❑ MISSING CLASS

Of course as an instructor I will tell you **never** miss class. I tell my students if I am doing my job, missing class will make things more difficult for you because I explain things and teach you things that will be hard to get from a book or difficult to understand without my presenting it to you. I can't teach you if you are not in my class.

I also tell my students this is the real world we are living in and when life happens, you may have to miss a class or two. *To stay out of the spot light and get the most from your instructor, treat your class the same as you would your job*. Isn't being a student really your job? Would you miss work and call in the next day to tell them you missed work yesterday? NO, sounds silly but all too frequently students miss class or even exams and fail to call or e-mail their instructor until several days later, if at all. What would happen if you did this at work? That's right; you would not have a job. Your instructor will not fire you or dismiss you from the class, but how willing do you think they are going to be to take their time to assist you when you need it if you keep missing their class? If you leave a message or e-mail your instructor **before** class, explain why you are not able to attend, and ask them to get in touch with you, most are usually very willing to assist you because you have demonstrated accountability and responsibility. Those behaviors get instructors all excited and willing to help. It really does not take a lot to keep us (instructors) happy and willing to bend over backwards to help you.

❑ PRACTICE CORRECT PRONUNCIATION

It is very difficult to memorize something you cannot pronounce. The first thing you have to do is learn how to pronounce something correctly. If you can speak it, you can memorize it much easier. Science (health care) is a foreign language; you have to practice speaking it *out loud*. Ask your instructor how to pronounce things correctly. You would not hesitate to ask in a language class, right? I can't emphasize this enough! Do this while you are studying at home and no one is around, or do it in your car. Just practice!

❑ STAY AWAKE!

Falling asleep is right up there with being late. Students who sleep in class usually fail right along with those who are consistently late. It can be a real challenge sometimes, especially if you work full time, work the night shift, have children, or any combination thereof, but

it is crucial. You cannot learn while you are asleep. I tried it in college and it did not work. I simply had to spend more time at home reading what I missed in class (not good time management). Here are a few things I have done over the years as a student to stay awake:

❑ **ALWAYS** sit in the front of the class! It is much harder to fall asleep and not pay attention the closer you are to the instructor. **NEVER** sit in the back. Think back to "How You Show Up" and what message it sends to your instructor when you sit in the front vs. the back? At some point you may need their help and isn't it in your best interest for them to have the best impression of you?

❑ Try not to dress so that you will become hot. It is human physiology to get tired and want to sleep if we are nice and warm. If the room is too warm, ask your instructor to turn down the temperature just a bit. You don't want to be cold either. Dress so that you can control your temperature. It is usually best to be ***comfortably cool***.

❑ If you can, avoid eating just before class, especially a big meal. Try—notice I say, ***try***—to get a good night's sleep before class. This is not always possible, but it does help. Remember why are you going to college? It is also good to remember it is costing someone money for you to sit in class. Nobody wants to waste money, especially your money.

❑ If allowed, bring a bottle of cold water (cold liquid) to class. Drinking a cold liquid helps keep you awake. If you really have trouble staying awake, this tip has worked well for me. Drink enough liquid before or during class that you will need to use the restroom by each break. It is difficult to sleep if you need to use the restroom.

If you are still falling asleep after trying all the above, you may need to excuse yourself from class to get a drink of water or do something; just take a break. Most instructors would rather have you take a quick **bathroom break** than sleep in their class. You may need to check on this with your instructor. You will actually miss much less class material by stepping out for just a few minutes than sleeping or sitting in class half-awake. The military allows students to stand at the back of the class rather than fall asleep. I encourage my students to do this. You may want to ask your instructor if it is an option. This has worked great for the military.

❑ ASK QUESTIONS

I know you have heard this a million times before, but it's true. And yes, it's also true that someone else usually has the same or similar question. Don't wait for someone else to ask the question because they may be doing the same thing, and then nobody asks the question! It's too late to ask questions on the exam. If you feel embarrassed to ask during class, wait until a break or after class to ask. If you don't ask your question, how are you going to feel if it shows up on the exam? *Seriously, do not let questions go unanswered. It will come back to bite you.*

❑ KEEP TRACK OF YOUR GRADE

If you have no idea what your grade is, how are you supposed to know how you are doing? How will you know how hard to study, if you can even pass the class, or how little you have to study to still maintain the grade you want? How would you know if your professor made a mistake in calculating your grade if you have not been tracking it? Let me ask you this: do most people balance their checkbook? Why? To make sure the bank does not make a mistake and to make sure you aren't overspending. The professor is far more likely to make a mistake entering hundreds of grades than the bank is calculating your balance electronically. The really nice thing is that you can figure your grades whenever you want, and as many times as you want. Even if your professor gives you grade reports throughout the course, don't be lazy and assume he or she will never make a mistake. It's your grade, and you should keep track of it. ***If you don't trust your bank to never make a mistake, why would you trust your instructor to never make one?*** It's not even about trust, it's about being human and to be human is to make mistakes. It's all too easy to hit the wrong key when entering hundreds of grades late at night, and who is going to catch the mistake if not you?

If you have not kept track of your grade and don't know how to figure it out, how are you going to determine what you need to get on the final or remaining exams to reach the grade you want/need? Example: If you know how to calculate your grade you can figure out exactly *to the percentage point* what you need on the final to achieve the grade you want, or if it's even possible to do so. ***Knowledge is power*** and wouldn't it be good to know going into the final that you could get a 40% on the exam and still maintain a B+? How do you think this might affect how you study for the exam? Well, you're not going to be stressed, are you? Maybe you have another class you are really worried about and now you have a lot more time you can dedicate to that class knowing what you now know. Wouldn't it be good to know going into the final that you will need a 125% to pass the class? "Yes, a 125% to pass the class, and no, that's not possible!" Unfortunately this has come up many times in my teaching career. A student finally gets it figured out (how to study and what needs to be done to be successful) and is super motivated to apply this newly discovered enthusiasm and right before the final and comes in to talk to me. I can tell they have not been tracking their grade because they are very excited and hopeful to take the final. It is very painful for me to say, "Do you remember how I showed you to track and figure your grade? You may want to do that ASAP." They are sad but very grateful I hinted that they needed to calculate their grade before studying for the final.

Along that same subject, if you do find yourself in this situation (needing a 125% on the final to pass) do not, repeat, **do not** skip the final unless you know you will never need to take and pass this class again. You have bought and paid for this class, and there is no refund at this point. You will have to take it again so why not give it your all even though you know you can't pass, just to get the experience? Here is a thought: if you like the instructor and plan on taking the class again, now you know what will be on the final. It is amazing how many students do this and score very high in this situation. I think telling them that they could not pass the course actually relieved all their anxiety while studying so that they retained so much more, and now they see what I am talking about with stress management and proper preparation. Together, we took a bad situation and made it into a very positive learning experience. ***If you cannot get your money back and you will need the class, never stop going and trying even if you know you can't pass!***

How to calculate your grade:

- Record **all** of your grades and the total possible points for each grade (see sample below).

- Keep track of both what it was worth and how many points you received.

- Make sure you record any missed assignments/quizzes as a zero.

- You will add up your total points and divide by the total possible points.

Use the following equation to calculate your grade.

$$\frac{\text{Your total points (add up ALL your homework's/quizzes/exams/extra credit)}}{\text{Total possible points (total points possible for homework/quizzes/exams)}} \times 100 = \text{percent (your grade)}$$

Homework/Quizzes (5 points each)	Exams (100 points each)
5	87
3	79
0	83
5	
4	
4	
21	+ 249 = 270

$$\frac{270}{330} = .8181 \times 100 = 81.8$$

This student is currently receiving an 82% for this class.

By recording this information, you can calculate your grade anytime you want. Most instructors can explain this further, if you have questions.

❑ REVIEW EXAMS

Always review your tests and assignments to figure out what you missed and why. It is not uncommon to see the same question more than once on exams and assignments. Avoid the temptation to just look at your score and leave early. If your instructor allows it, you should take notes on what you missed on the exam. If your instructor does not allow you to do this, then immediately after class write down any questions you can remember that you missed. Review them before the next exam. This tip is especially important when there is a comprehensive exam. Most instructors allow you to review your exam, but you may have to ask.

❑ OLD EXAMS

If you do a little looking and asking around, you can frequently find old exams from your instructor. If possible, review them. They can do several things for you. The most important is get you accustomed to how the instructor likes to ask questions and their style so you are not surprised on the first exam. One of the most difficult things about the first exam for every class is to discover the instructor's testing style and how they express themselves. Reviewing previous exams can really help with this. Furthermore, you get practice taking tests on the subject matter, which is always helpful, especially for those who are not good at taking tests.

Finally, you never know how many questions you may see repeated on different exams. I should not tell you this but I had a chemistry teacher who had about seven different versions of his exams. A friend had a file on this professor that he passed on to me. One of the exams was exactly the same, word-for-word, that I had been using to review with. You can imagine my delight at this discovery! Yes, I received an A+ on that exam and probably would have without this added assistance. I was just very confident before even looking at the results the next week. That's not cheating; if your professors allow students to keep their exams, this can and should be expected to happen. As the Marines would say, *"Improvise, Adapt, and Overcome."* Be honest and honorable, but by all means exploit an opportunity if it presents itself. This is the very reason I do not let my students keep their tests!

❏ BE ORGANIZED AND "QUIET PLEASE"

Study in a clean and organized location. Being organized is time efficient. Having a clean study area provides fewer distractions. This tip seems like, and is, common sense. Just remember, the less time you have to spend studying, the more time you have to play.

Many students think that background noise such as music or television helps them, or are simply in the habit of studying this way. However, research shows this is not the most efficient way to study (remember) because it interferes with concentration. The more things that are going on around you, both visually and auditory, the more they distract your brain and decrease your concentration abilities. If you had to take an exam in similar circumstances (loud background noise and lots of movement going on around you) then I would say by all means, you should study this way, but this is not the case. It is always best to practice how you will perform. This is why the military practices with all kinds of loud noises and things going on to distract you, because this is the environment in which you will be performing. What will the environment be like where you take your exam? Find a clean, organized, and *quite* place to do your studying. You will retain more and need less time to do it. With that said, everyone is different and a few people can actually concentrate better with particular types of music. Know yourself and know what works for you!

Being organized also means knowing what you are supposed to be doing and when. Get a planner or use a calendar. I like Google calendar (or something similar) because it's on my computer and links up with my smart phone to let me know when I need to be doing something. The options are endless! This is a **perfect** example of using technology correctly when it comes to studying and learning.

❑ "TO DO LISTS"

While taking a leadership course in the Navy, a very prominent Naval Captain was speaking to our unit about the importance of to do lists. He stated that most every successful officer used to do lists and encouraged us to do so. I definitely agree with him and give you the same advice. This is one of the most important tools you can employ in life to keep focused and successful. It is invaluable for students. I highly recommend having two different lists. I have my long-term list on my computer desktop called "TO DO LIST." On this list I keep all items that will take more than a few days, up to several months. The idea is to list things that I might forget while working on more important or short-term goals. Here is what my "TO DO LIST" looks like at the moment of writing this:

TO DO LIST

1.   **Plan College Bootcamps for fall terms**
2.   **Create daily reminders for classes**
3.   **Collect data on RN's for AHEC**
4.   **Update fall syllabus and Bb**
5.   **Update schools e-mail list**
6.   **Compare and fix PMR**

Now most of this will not make sense to you, but it does to me. None of these things need to be done today. In fact, many are not due for several weeks or even months. The point is it only needs to make sense to me. I keep it saved on my desktop in a Word file. I look at it once every day or two to see if there is anything that needs to be on my *Today list*.

My *Today list* consists of a post-it pad. That's right, a yellow post-it pad. I like this for several reasons. Each day, I physically write what I want to get done that day. I think there is something about using actual paper and pen, and then I also get to draw a line through each task as I complete it. I have no  research to prove or back this, but I think there is really something to being able to physically check off each item that increases motivation and provides a sense of accomplishment, which leads to completing the list each day. At the end of the day I get to pull off the top sheet, crunch it up in my hand, and throw it way. If I did not finish the list, I leave it and the next morning when I get to my office, I pull it off and copy any items left from the day before to the top of today's list. The post-it pad allows you to "post-it" anywhere you like. Sometimes I have it on the dash of my car if I am traveling for business. There are many ways of doing this, I just like the old pen and paper and being able to throw the list away each day. It gives me a sense of accomplishment! *HINT: Do not put things on your daily yellow post-it To-Do-List that can't possibly be done in one day. Example: write 30-page thesis paper today. Instead, put "work on paper today." It's ok to put lots of separate smaller items on this list even if you know you can't get them all done that day. Put them in the order you want them accomplished and transfer what's left at the end of the day to the next day. Most of the time, I only put down what I can accomplish in that day.*

❑ TEAM EFFORT

"There is no 'i' in team but there is in win" – Michael Jordan

Try studying with someone from your class or in a group. This can be very beneficial because it can provide a different perspective after sitting through the same class maybe even introducing something you missed or forgot. As beneficial as this can be, if not done correctly it can be extremely nonproductive and a massive waste of time. If you do try studying with a group, you have to stay on track. Have a plan before meeting and set some ground rules. Know what it is you are going to accomplish before getting together. You may even want to designate someone to be the "monitor" to make sure you stick to the plan. One effective exercise is to have everyone bring their flash cards and take turns quizzing the group. If you do not have flash cards, then have each person look through his or her notes and ask the others questions that might be on the exam. If an individual does not contribute to the group or is distracting, ask him or her to leave, or simply do not invite the person again. **Warning**: it is really easy to get together and complain about the class and be nonproductive. This may feel good, but it won't get you the grade you want!

❏ READ THE TEXTBOOK

Many instructors give students handouts or notes, and I have heard students say, "All you have to do is follow their handouts." This may work for some, but not for all. Your grade usually dictates whether it is working for you. There is a reason the instructor has chosen the text. You can still focus most of your energy on the instructor's notes, but you need to use the text to fill in the gaps. Class handouts and notes are meant to be a guide so that you know what you should read in the text. It is usually not the expectation that you read the text from cover to cover. In fact, I usually discourage students from doing this because they tend to get lost and lose focus on what the class is covering. Too much information can be distracting. This is why I recommend attending lecture prior to reading the text. You should *skim* the text before coming to class, but this is not the same as reading it. Skimming is just looking through the chapters, seeing what is there, how things are laid out, and knowing where things are in your book. When you skim, mark the chapters that you will be covering in class and will be on the next exam with a post-it or small piece of paper. Now they even make these little stickies just for this.

Once you have skimmed and marked your chapters, take your text to the lecture with you. You may or may not use it depending on the instructor and their style. In classes with charts and diagrams, you will certainly want to have those pages marked so you can view them and mark them in your text as the instructor covers them. I say more about this later in the book.

After the lecture, you should have a good idea about what it is that you should be looking for or focusing on in the text. Now go back and read your text! I highly encourage students to highlight in the text when they read it. See the following section on how to get the most out of highlighting.

Most textbooks are very busy with all kinds of hints, tips, "know this" sections, case studies, examples, boxes and diagrams. Sometimes these are great, other times they may not be so helpful and may even be distracting. Figure out what is helpful and what is not. Look for sample test questions or quizzes at the end of the chapters. They are always good to take, because you can never get enough practice taking tests. In classes that have problems to solve like math, chemistry, and physics, ***do any and all of them that you will be expected to do!*** If you know you do not have to do a particular type of problem, ***don't do it***. Focus on the ones you will be expected to know. When you first start reading a textbook, it will be a slow learning process, as you will read everything. You will quickly figure out what is important and useful and what is not, and then you will be able to read much more efficiently and effectively. No instructor seriously expects you to read the text word-for-word from front to back, so don't even try. This is why I consistently keep referring to learning and studying as an Art. It takes intent and practice to get really good at it but WOW, the time you can save while actually doing better is well worth your effort.

A new thing that colleges are doing is renting textbooks. From the college's perspective, this is another way to make money. If you are a student, I would not recommend this. You need to be able to **use you textbook** and this means highlighting and writing in it. I tracked this for several years and found that students who wrote and highlighted in their textbooks earned much higher grades than students who did not because they were worried about the "resale value" of their textbooks when the class was over. The class itself costs a lot more than the textbook, and for most colleges, used is used. It makes no difference whether you mark in it or not, you get the same amount of money back.

❑ THE ART OF HIGHLIGHTING

I recommend that when you skim (prior to going to class) you do not highlight **anything**. You are just reading (skimming) to have an idea about what will be covered and hopefully increasing your chances of retention from class. Again, don't **read** before the lecture, **skim** the chapter. Sometimes it may be necessary to actually read the material before the lecture. Your instructor will usually inform you if this is the case. After class you will have a much better idea what is important and what will be on the exam. This is the time to read the text and highlight what was covered that you **do not** already know or have put to memory. What do I mean by this? **Avoid** highlighting what you already know and will remember. The idea of highlighting is to bring to your attention what you will need to know but **don't** have memorized. You can go back later and highlight your highlights of what you still can't remember. You should only have to read the chapter from start to finish **ONCE!** You highlight the important stuff (again, things you do not know or have memorized) the first time through to complete your notes. You go back later after studying or making flash cards and read just what you highlighted the first time. You will have committed to memory much of what you highlighted the first time, and now you highlight only the things that you still do not have memorized. Use a different color to track what you still need to memorize. You can do this several times until you have a firm grasp of everything that is necessary. This way you can review the required chapters in the text in a very short amount of time.

❏ BEFORE COMING TO CLASS

You should always come to class having some idea of what you are going to learn about that day. You can't expect to walk out of class understanding everything that was presented even if you did read the text prior to class. However, you will retain much more information if you come to class prepared. All you need to do is *skim* the book or notes before class, and then read the book after class when you have an idea what to focus on. Skimming should take only about twenty minutes for each class. This may vary depending on the class and what is to be covered.

❏ COVER-UNCOVER TEST

This is for subjects that have images or diagrams such as anatomy, physiology, etc. Highlight the pictures/diagrams in the text that are covered in class. Be sure to highlight only the things that you will be required to know for lab or lecture exams and quizzes, and ***do not forget*** to highlight some of the line that points to the structure being identified. This way, if you cover the names with a note card or your hand, you will be able to tell what lines need to be identified.

Go to the diagram you want to learn, and cover the names of the structures on the picture with a note card or your hand. Say out loud all the structures indicated by highlighted lines. Remove the note card or your hand, and see how many of the structures you identified correctly. Immediately cover the names if you missed any, and do all of them again. Repeat several times until you can identify them all correctly, and then move to another picture.

It should take you only a few minutes to cover each picture. Do this multiple times a day. The more *frequently* you do this, the faster you will be able to memorize. I have heard many professors say, "Anatomy is more than memorization. The students can't just memorize the material; they need to know how to apply it." Anatomy is the same as geography: maps showing locations of things in relation to each other. I would argue the best way to learn a map is looking at a map, over and over.

I don't think most people would find it very helpful to read the description of locations on a map. Learning a map is pretty much straight-up memorization. I would suggest that the best way to initially learn anatomy is to discover the best way for you to memorize. Once you have the basics of anatomy memorized, then and only then can you begin to apply the information and make connections. This goes for all subjects. The memorization must come first. Memorizing is not that complicated. The key is repetition, and the cover-uncover test is fast, efficient, and very effective.

I tell my students this can even be done while watching their favorite TV program. Have your text with the proper pages flagged and the pictures highlighted. Sit down to watch your favorite one-hour TV program. At the first commercial break, open your text to the flagged page and do the cover-uncover test until the commercial is over. Put down your text and let your mind take a break. This actually works really well because you let your mind relax by focusing on your TV show. In about ten minutes you will have another commercial, allowing you to study again. I recommend you mute the TV during the commercial breaks. You will have about five or six mini study sessions while watching your TV program. Students are **SHOCKED, AMAZED,** and **PERPLEXED** as to how effective this actually is. You can do this while cleaning the house, putting away dishes, doing laundry, etc. It seems crazy to even suggest this, but it really works. The great thing is you can take this study concept and apply it to breaks at work, when you get up in the morning before breakfast, after breakfast, etc. Who cannot spare three or four minutes several times a day? If you use flash cards, you can do the same thing. This is the most efficient and effective way I have discovered to put massive amounts of data to memory in the shortest time possible. Again, you have to put it to memory before you can start to use it, apply it, and make connections. You *must* try this. It really does work!

❑ QUANTITY VS. QUALITY

You should understand the terms "quantity" and "quality" in connection with how they relate to studying. We are taught and grow up believing that more is better. However, more studying (increased quantity) is not necessarily better or more effective. In fact, it is very time inefficient and nonproductive. Most of the time, longer study sessions will cause the quality to decrease. The fact is that *quality* is almost always more important than *quantity*. The same can be said about exercise, and research has proven it. As you study for a period of time, the quality is best at the beginning, and then decreases as time goes on. The solution to this is to increase the quantity of study sessions and make the sessions shorter, thus increasing the quality of the sessions. For example, you will remember (memorize) more information with six fifteen-minute study sessions rather than one three-hour session. Do the math: you will spend less time overall and be more effective with frequent, shorter study sessions. This seems too good to be true, so what is the secret? You can't do this at the last minute. You need to do this all along, throughout the week, for this to work. You cannot do this if you "cram."

❑ DON'T CRAM

Some students can get away with this, but most cannot. **"CRAMMING"** does **NOT** work! Students who can cram for a course like anatomy and do well are exceptional and natural memorizers. If cramming will work for you, you are already aware of your natural ability to memorize. However, I still do not recommend it. You could spend less time studying and get the same or better grade by not cramming.

You will actually spend less time overall if you study a little bit every day rather than if you wait until just before the test to begin to study. In addition, you will usually have significantly less perceived stress by doing a little bit every day. One last thing to consider is that waiting to study at the last minute can have serious consequences. Let's say you wait until the weekend to study for a Monday or Tuesday exam. What are you going to do if something comes up unexpectedly over the weekend? I have a feeling this would explain many of the "sick" calls I get on Monday mornings for my Monday exams.

This is probably the hardest of all the rules to follow. The best time to study is right after the material is presented in class or as soon as possible (within twenty-four hours) while the information is still fresh in your mind. If you wait too long, it is like reading it for the first time and requires much more time. After all, your goal is to learn as much as possible, and earn the best grade with as little effort as possible. What I am saying is you don't want to make it any harder than it has to be. You can greatly increase your grade and almost cut your study time in half if you do this.

❏ TAKING NOTES

Don't try to write down everything the instructor tells you. Most of us cannot write and really listen at the same time. If you are one of those who write everything down, think how often you leave class and really have no idea what was said. This is not to say that you should not take any notes, but if you have skimmed the material prior to class, you will recall reading it, and after class you can easily find it in the text or notes and highlight what was important. I have found I get far more out of the lecture if I just listen and take few, if any, notes. However, I need to read the text fairly soon and highlight important points mentioned in lecture in the text. I use the text as my notes. If you do not follow through with highlighting the text, then you must take thorough notes in class or you will forget information presented in lecture.

If you are someone who must take notes because that is your learning style, learn to be efficient when taking notes. Do not write down every word. If you have a good text and the instructor uses the text, you can frequently just write down key words or phrases to remind yourself what to look up later when you have time. For example, if the instructor is describing nerve impulse conduction just write "Describe nerve impulse conduction" in your notes. If the instructor describes five steps they want you to know, write "1-5" below, and then write key words to describe each step to help you remember later. Avoid writing whole complete sentences and try to keep your notes short and simple. Most students retain more when they are able to actually listen to the lecture rather than focusing their attention on writing. Taking notes is most definitely an individual art and you will need to do some *trial-and-error*. Find a group of students (I recommend students that are doing well) and compare notes. This will help you fill in the gaps and also give you many different examples of note taking to help you find *your* method.

❏ EXAM PREPARATION

Prepare for an exam as though the exam date were several days **before** the actual exam. For example, if your exam is on a Friday, study and prepare as though the exam is on Wednesday. "Why would I do this?" How many times have you gone into exams thinking, "If only I had another day"? When you prepare for an exam you inevitably realize before the exam that there are some areas that need more work. By doing this, you have given yourself those few extra days to finalize your preparation.

For this to really work, you **MUST** prepare as though the test were really two or three days sooner than it actually is. This does not take any more of your time. You are simply moving the timetable up two days. It gives you two or three days of **easy** review and **dramatically** decreases anxiety. Students always tell me "I have terrible anxiety before and during a test; my mind goes blank." This is usually due to finding those areas of weakness just before the test and wishing that they had a few more days to study.

"Spectacular achievement is always preceded by unspectacular preparation" – Robert H. Schuller

You want to walk into a test feeling confident and ready to unload or regurgitate all the information floating around in your mind. It should be a relief to take a test, not a horrifying experience. Most test-taking anxiety arises from being unprepared. Being prepared in advance will also help to prevent any temptation to cram. This is another one that I have had a difficult time convincing my students to try, but it really works. I did this this all the way through graduate school. Just try it one time and you will be hooked!

❑ COMPREHENSIVE EXAMS

If your class has a comprehensive exam, **do not** quit studying material covered by the previous exams. It's much like exercising. It takes a lot of time and energy to get into shape, but less effort to stay in shape. It took you time and energy to learn the material for the first exam. Now all you have to do are minor reviews to keep the material fresh in your mind for the final exam. If you don't do this, you will find yourself spending a lot of time and energy relearning the same material at the end of the course. You deserve to enjoy college life and be a student at the same time. Why make it harder than it has to be?

Be sure to read "Strategic Studying" below and apply the same concept here when preparing for comprehensive exams. It could actually save your grade to not study a particular chapter or section on the upcoming final or comprehensive exam.

❑ **MAKE FLASH CARDS**

See "The Art of Making Flash Cards" section

❑ **WHERE TO STUDY**

Study in a comfortable and quiet atmosphere. Limit distractions as much as possible. Studying is not a test of your multitasking skills. Try to plan this out in advance, and schedule your study time when you will have the fewest distractions. One more reason that *quantity* versus *quality* is very effective is that it is much simpler to find many short time periods to study without distractions, rather than one big chunk of time. For many people, this may mean using the library or getting up before others do.

❑ **WHEN TO STUDY**

The best time to study is when you are the most awake and alert. This will vary from person to person and will be determined by their biorhythm. I am a morning person. The best time for me to start studying is 5:30-6:00 a.m. I usually get sleepy and start to lose focus around 7:00 p.m. I figured this out early in college and always did most of my studying in the morning when I was the most efficient and effective. If I had continued to try to study at night with most of my friends, it would have taken up a lot more of my time and would still not have been as effective. Know yourself and use that knowledge to pick the best times to study for you. Obviously, you will find it very difficult to create a study group at 5:30 a.m., but you can usually get people to do it later in the afternoon or very early in the evening.

Try not to study after eating a meal. It is physiology to want to go to sleep after eating and this is frequently not the best time to study. It is best to plan ahead when you are going to study and to have a set start and stop time (review setting goals if you need to). Plan out all the details or, at the very least, think about what your goal is before you start studying. Don't just study when it seems like a good time, plan it out to make the most of your time.

❑ ASK FOR HELP

Don't be afraid to ask for help! If you are following the above advice and still not doing well, it does you no good to go to your instructor the last couple of weeks before the final exam and say, "I don't think I am doing well." Ask for help as soon as you realize you are not doing well. Ask for help with enough time left in the course that you can actually make a difference. If you ask too late, what is the point? You don't have enough time left to make a difference. What have you got to lose? Don't wait!

❑ UNDERSTANDING SUCCESS

The most important of all the suggestions and ideas I can give you is to make sure you understand the *first tip listed on the checklist, Understanding Success*. Go back and read it again and make sure you understand it. You get out of classes what you put into them!

❑ STRATEGIC STUDYING

In a perfect world you will have enough time to study everything that needs to be studied. However this is reality and in the real world we often find ourselves in a pinch, and do not have all the time we need. If you have an exam coming up and you only have five hours that you can use to study, but you know it is going to take seven hours to cover **all** the material, you need to make some choices. Simple math dictates something will have to get less attention. This is where strategic studying comes in.

If there is a chapter that you are weak in but there will only be a few questions on the exam that relate to this material, skip it so that you may spend your time studying chapters that will have the most questions. I call this strategic studying because you are going to sacrifice that material on the exam in order to allow you to do better in other areas and to increase your chances of success. If you really put some thought into this, you can usually figure out what needs to be sacrificed. I don't recommend asking your instructor unless you know they would be open to this kind of question and will give you a helpful response. You may want to feel them out. If they are not receptive, this approach might work against you. If they are, their response could be **tremendously** helpful.

It is always best to prepare so that you never have to use this strategy, but something will eventually come up and using it could decrease your stress and save your grade. It is a valuable *emergency* strategy to have thought about before needing to employ it. It also can be very helpful in taking comprehensive exams with limited time to study.

❏ PRACTICE PERFORING UNDER STRESS AND TIME LIMITS

I have frequently had students come to me and say, "I don't understand, I knew the material before the exam and my grade does not reflect that." If they knew the material, it should have been reflected in their score. Are they lying? No, but something is definitely wrong. It could be one of many things or a combination of factors. The most common cause for this feeling is because when students read their notes they make perfect sense. However *reading* and *recalling* information are two totally different things. To make sure you are able to recall information, the use of flash cards can prove invaluable (see section on flash cards). Assume the student really was appropriately prepared. Why did they not do well on the exam? The answer usually is one of two things: they do not perform well on exams, or they do not perform well with a time limit and under stress. (It's possibly a combination of both.) If the problem is test taking, see the section on *The Art of Test Taking*.

Let's focus on stress and time. This is not an uncommon problem, but is often is not properly addressed. Wishing that you get better at taking timed tests without getting stressed is not going to help. "So what do I do?" you ask. The answer is so simple it's ridiculous. If you are bad at taking timed tests and get stressed, how do you get better?....... *Take more timed tests and practice under stressful conditions.* You do not want to practice this while you are taking tests that actually count towards your grade. Get as many sample exams as you can find in the subject matter. Often instructors have old exams they would be happy to let you practice with. Other students may have old exams. After you get the old tests, don't just look them over, take them with the same time limit you will have in class. The only way to get better is practice, practice, and more practice!

Another method to help with stress is to use a study partner. Get together and have them drill you two days before the exam. You should be prepared to take the exam before you meet and have nothing left to do but review (not study – see test taking strategies). Have your partner rake you over the coals, grill you, drill you, and stress you out while asking you questions. The idea is to get you used to taking an exam while feeling stressed. It will be much simpler to take the exam in a nice quiet room than it is with someone drilling you with short answer questions. The military has understood this concept for decades. You will perform under stress to your lowest level of training, so practice until it becomes muscle memory. For whatever reason, most of us do not take this approach when practicing for exams. We just expect that we will get better and you do but at what expense when your practice is on actual class exams?

❏ WHAT TO TAKE NOTES ON/IN?

I think the best thing to take notes in is a three-ring binder. Some would say that is old-school but it's really more about the effectiveness than a habit. The three-ring is cheap, easy to refill, add to, rearrange, and reuse for taking notes. Spiral bound note pads that you have to tear the paper out of just don't work as well. They are messy and many instructors will not accept paper with all the "frills" on the side, or require you to remove them. Trust me, just go with the three-ring and you will be much happier.

Another thing to mention is always bring your textbook to class. Some even like to use their textbook to take notes in. The one thing it is superb for is a diagram. Human anatomy, for example, has a lot of diagrams and pictures and most instructors will use the very same pictures and diagrams from your book. Because they are covering what they want you to know on these diagrams, you can simply highlight them in your textbook. Quick and simple!

❏ "PROBLEM" BASED CLASSES

Classes like math, chemistry, and physics involve solving and balancing equations. The approach to these classes is going to be very different from the way you are going to approach English 101. There is a lot of memorization involved in these classes and unfortunately flash cards will have limited use. After making sure you understand or have memorized all definitions and values that you will need, it's **just practice, practice, practice, and more practice!** Find every example of the types of questions or equations you will be expected to take on an exam and solve them. This is where the textbook and online recourses can really help. More than any other class, tutors can prove to be extremely helpful along, with frequent visits with the instructor to answer your questions. If you do not understand how to do a problem, you had better get it figured out because there is no guessing on these types of questions. Frequent practice is the key to success, and procrastination and cramming in these types of courses is almost certain to result in failure! You must start strong and never fall behind because once you do it is **extremely** difficult to catch up, and students rarely do. You will sink or swim in these classes but they are good for students because they teach you some very valuable lessons: do not procrastinate, and cramming is your enemy

THE ART OF TEST TAKING

"Accept the challenges so that you can feel the exhilaration of victory" – George S. Patton

Just like studying, there is definitely an art to taking tests. A person who understands how to take tests can achieve scores of 50% or better even when they know nothing about the tested material. It's true! How? By learning "The Art of Test Taking." Many books have been written on the subject of test taking, and there are even more suggestions. The following are some things that I have learned over the years that worked for me and seem to be at the core of every test-taking book. Unfortunately, there is no secret to taking tests. As you just learned, more is not always better, quality is what is the most important, and that goes for study tips too! However, all the tips in the world will not replace proper preparation.

There are many types of exam questions: fill in the blank, true/false, matching, essay, short answer, and multiple choice. Let's do a quick review of each:

Fill in the blank – This is the highest level of difficulty for test questions. Either you know it or you don't. Unlike essay questions, you can't even try to make something sound good or make it sound like you know what you are talking about. If all else fails you should put down the first thing that pops into your head. Never leave them blank.

True/False – LOL, students love to see these on exams, and for good reason. These are the lowest level of test question and you have a 50/50 chance of getting them right. I am surprised when I see these on college exams. Again, the first thing that pops into you mind is usually the correct answer.

Matching – A tip for answering matching questions is to approach them in same way as a fill in the blank. Most of the time matching involves linking a definition to the term. When you look at the term, think about what its definition is, and then look for the answer. Always start with the answers you know first and leave the ones you are unsure of or don't know for last.

Essay and short answer – This is not just about answering a question; it is also about your writing skills. First and foremost, you need to sound professional and scholarly. Do not use slang and improper English! How you write your and presentation of the material can potentially make up for some lack of subject matter knowledge. You could also have an adequate knowledge base and be very well prepared, but if you can't properly present your thoughts you may lose points. If you are not good at essay questions, I strongly suggest you contact your instructor to see if they can help you improve your writing skills. One of the best ways to do this is to see if the instructor will allow you to give him/her a few samples before the exam so you can get some feedback and make necessary changes in the way you present your information. The only way to improve your essay writing skills is through practice.

Multiple choice – This is the most common form of question used on exams related to the sciences, healthcare, and any subject where material needs to memorized. The remainder of this section mostly refers to multiple choice questions and general test taking tips.

The following is a list of proven test taking tips that have been used by my students and by me for years with great success. Use this as a checklist to see what you have been doing and what you may want to try.

"Sound strategy starts with having the right goal" – Michael Porter

❏ "READ THE DIRECTIONS!!!"

You would not believe how many points I have seen lost over the years because the student did not read the directions. Every time you take an exam, you should read the directions. Most instructors will deduct points for not following directions, or may not give any credit at all. For example, most math and chemistry courses will not give credit if you don't show all your work. These are the most painful of all points to be lost on an exam so, to avoid the pain, read the directions.

❏ TEST QUESTION "GIVE-AWAYS"

Many instructors give away as much as 25% of their test questions, some even more. I make a point to mention every single test question in class so the students have good reason to attend my lectures and pay attention. I tell them this the first day of class and I even tell them the things to watch for that gives the test questions away. What's on the test is not supposed to be a secret. I also tell my students many things that are not on the test. They get what they want and I get what I want: they pay attention to what I am saying while looking for clues about what is really important and likely to be on the test.

Here is what I tell them:

- *Listen for the topic of stories.* Many instructors get off on side subjects but if they start telling a story that relates to the topic of discussion, you can almost guarantee you will see it on the exam. Why are we telling you a story? Because we think it's an important topic and are trying to give you an example of how it relates to or shows up in the real world and, of course, this is going through our minds when writing the test.

- *Repeating ourselves!* I just mentioned a term three different times in a short period of time. Do you think I think that's important? What am I most likely to populate my tests with? Important things I think you need to know, or irrelevant things I don't even bother to mention? Exactly, we are not senile and forgetting what we just said, we are trying to give you a hint! ☺

- ***Think like your instructor.*** Try to get in their head and think like them. The problem for many students in preparing for exams is they are thinking like a student. Don't focus on what *you* think is important, or even worse, what you would like to see on the test. Focus on what you think the *instructor* thinks is important. The only way you are going to know that is by attending class and listening for the clues and giveaways. When writing this book, I am thinking like a student and that is why some of the things I tell you are a little off the wall and not "Professor-like." It works both ways. Let's use it to our advantage in working together.

- ***Don't miss the obvious!*** When we say, "you really need to know this, this is important, don't forget, etc." or we say something loudly, slowly, or repeat it, the material should be flagged and marked in your notes or text! ***Don't let "freebies" get away!*** Whenever I heard any of the above, I always put a big "*" right next it in my notes. Lots of students like to put TQ (for *test question*) right next to it in their notes. Just ***do something*** so you know this is a highly probable test question.

- ***Compare with others.*** Before or after each class, review what was covered in the last lecture for these clues. You may have gone to the restroom or simply drifted off to a "happy place" for a moment and missed a giveaway. Compare with other students and you will get almost every single one. You may just be shocked at how much you correctly predicted was on your test! This is most definitely a skill worth developing.

❏ DON'T PICK ME!

AVOID answers that have the words **"NEVER," "ALWAYS,"** and **"ALL."** This does not work 100 % of the time, but statistically it is in your favor to avoid that answer if you are unsure of the correct answer. Only go with one of these answers if you used the next method to answer it. *Absolutes are rarely true!*

❏ MULTIPLE-CHOICE OR SHORT ANSWER?

Treat all multiple-choice questions as if they were short answer. By this I mean read the question and *do not look at the answers*. You may even want to bring a blank three-by-five note card to cover the answers (make sure you clear this with your instructor first). Try to answer the question, and then look for your answer in your options. If you find your answer in the ones provided, **STOP** and do not read the others. What frequently happens is that when students look at the other options, they will talk themselves out of the correct answer.

If you are unable to answer the question with the method above, look at the answers provided. Maybe seeing the answer will trigger your memory. If this still does not generate the correct answer in your mind, **LEAVE IT!** Yes, *LEAVE IT!* Make a notation on your test booklet (if you are allowed to write on your test) and come back to it later. Many times you will find the answer in another question or remember while answering other questions. *"The clock is ticking."* Just don't forget to go back and answer it. *Only* do this if it is possible to come back to questions later! This mostly applies to paper and pencil tests. If your exam is an electronic test you will want to be very clear if you can do this before starting the exam. Many online or electronic exams do not let you go back to previous questions. Ask your instructor before starting the exam. If you cannot go back and answer it later or you have come back to it for the third time and still don't know the answer, cross out the answers you **know** (without doubt) are **incorrect** and see what is left. Typically this leaves only one or two answers. If this still does not generate the correct answer in your mind, you will have to make an educated choice. In other words, *give it your best guess* and that is usually your first "gut" feeling. Never leave a question blank; a guess is better than nothing. *Note: I have run across a few very strange methods of grading exams were every possible answer on a multiple choice test counts. This is a very uncommon method of grading exams and I discovered that on those exams it is better to leave blank what you are unsure of. I would not worry about this too much; in eight years of school I only encountered it once.*

❑ ESSAY QUSTIONS

I will be the first to admit that essay questions were not my strong suit, and in some ways that may make my advice even better. You want to keep your essay short and to the point. Many students try to hide their lack of knowledge in more words and think they can trick the instructor into believing that they actually know what they are talking about....try again. All you will accomplish is annoying the instructor because you just wasted a bunch of their time reading garbage.

Make sure to include a brief introduction, body, and conclusion. The introduction is simply stating the issue you intend to answer or address and maybe a little background information. The body is where you make your case. The body is where you answer the question. This is where you prove that you know what you are talking about. Make sure it is written professionally and that it sounds intelligent. Never use slang or improper English in your essay. Keep your answer focused, organized, and supported with facts or figures if possible. The conclusion is your final statement to the question and your answer. It should be a very brief summary of what you just proved or answered.

If you are like me and do not like essay questions, make sure you are well prepared for them. Talk to your instructor before the exam and see if you can get samples of their expectations or of "good" student essays from them. Ask for help and be prepared. To prepare for an essay exam is going to be very different than preparing for a standard multiple-choice exam. I think one of the best ways is getting a study group together and practice by taking turns giving the other students essay type questions that would most likely be on the test. You can either write the questions out and then read them aloud or answer them out loud to the group, and then get feedback and have open discussion on each person's answer. The more you can practice and get feedback from someone else, preferably someone who is good at essay writing, the better.

❑ LEAVE THE WORST FOR LAST

I know, you have been told don't procrastinate and don't leave the classes you fear are the hardest until last, but when it comes to taking a test, *if possible*, always leave the most difficult questions until last. They will take the most time and you want to correctly answer as many other "easy" questions as you can first. It makes perfect sense if you really think about it. Get as many quick and easy questions as you can in case you run out of time.

❏ NEED FOR SPEED

I recommend that the first time through, take the test as quickly as possible. When I say as quickly as possible, I don't mean it is a race, but you don't want to stop on any one question very long for several reasons. Most exams are timed, and you don't want to run out of it. The typical exam is 60-100 questions and it is not uncommon to be given an hour to take it. That means you have 60 seconds or less per question. That is not a lot of time and the more time you spend on any one question, the less you will have for others.

When you get to each question either you know it or you don't. You want to answer all the questions you know for sure (without a doubt). This keeps your confidence up and your mind focused. It is better to come back to questions that you are unsure of. Sitting and staring at the same question for several minutes only increases anxiety. Anxiety only makes things worse and impairs memory. It would not be unusual to have skipped as much as 30-50% of the exam, again, you *only* answered the questions you were 100% sure of. That is ok; you now know what is on the exam. You have looked at every question and can now assess how much time you have left compared to what needs a second look. This is a very strategic approach to taking an exam and maximizes your time for each question. It also keeps anxiety to a minimum by not allowing you the time to get yourself worked up.

Once you have finished the exam, go back and answer all the questions you left blank. You can even try the same thing again a second time: answer the ones you can and leave the ones you don't know blank to come back to a third time. *Remember: your first guess is usually the correct one. You don't want to give yourself time to talk yourself out of the correct answer. That's why I call it the need for speed!*

❏ USING A BUBBLE SHEET?

If you can write on the test booklet, answer **ALL** the questions on the booklet first, and when you're completely finished, go back and transfer your answers to the bubble sheet. This should be the last thing you do before turning in your exam. Look it over to make sure it is all filled in correctly (including your name and anything else needed) and do one last double check with your exam book to make sure the correct bubbles are filled in for each question.

Doing this saves you time and prevents mistakes from constantly going back and forth. Also, it keeps you from correcting errors on your bubble or scanner sheet where making corrections can cause the computer to make errors grading your paper.

❏ YOUR GUT FEELING

Usually your first thought is the correct one. In other words, **DON'T** change an answer unless you are 110% sure your first answer was incorrect. I can't stress this one enough. If you are answering the questions the way I previously suggested, then don't change your answers. Statistics shows this to be true when you are unsure. If it was a mistake, absolutely change your answer.

❑ 1-2 HOURS BEFORE THE EXAM

Do not study an hour before the exam. I usually recommend not even looking at the material an hour before the exam. This only increases anxiety and is not productive. If you do not know the material an hour before the exam, you did not prepare properly and may actually do worse by last minute studying. This is the hardest concept to get students to believe and practice because of the one or two answers they get right due to that last minute studying. What they don't realize is how many questions they potentially missed because of doing this. You want to work out of your *long term* memory, not *short term*. Trust me on this one. If you have followed my suggestions for the Art of Studying, there is no need for **studying** the day of the test, only **reviewing**. Even reviewing right before the exam usually causes an increase in anxiety. Really think about it, what are you going to learn or memorize in the few minutes before the exam begins?

❑ DON'T ADD TO THE QUESTIONS!

Be sure not to add words to the questions or answers. It is not a good idea to say to yourself, "This would be right if..." or "This could be right if..." *Read the questions and answers as they are written* and avoid talking yourself into the answer. Students do this all the time and are not even aware that they are doing it until they come to discuss the questions with me and they add words while discussing it. I have to remind them, "That was not the question on the test." You really have to be careful if you are one of those students who do this.

If you have to justify the answer in your mind, you have probably talked yourself into the answer, and it is usually the wrong answer. If you have problems with this, I recommend you use the three-by-five note card to cover your choices as the second suggestion recommends. It has helped many of my students to stop doing this. **Remember:** *you are choosing the correct answer according to your instructor, not according to you.*

❏ THERE IS NO 1ST PLACE

Use all the time given. There is no rush to finish first nor is there a reward for doing so. Yes, you want to get through the exam as quickly as possible the **FIRST** time. This is so you do not read more into the questions and so that you have time to go back and answer the ones you were unsure of. It is also a good idea to double-check your answers for simple mistakes. If done properly, you should finish the exam just before time is up. In my experience, the students who are done first either did exceptionally well or really bad. Besides, who cares about them? This is your test and your time—use it.

❏ PUT IT ON PAPER

If you learned any mnemonics and can write on the test, you should write them out on the exam as soon as you get it. **Do not wait!** You do not want to take the chance that anxiety causes you to forget them. I tell my students to write and draw all over the test if allowed. You may even want to draw diagrams and charts and label them before you get started. This is **extremely** helpful in courses such as anatomy and physiology. Quickly create your own cheat-sheet (on the test itself) from memory **before** starting the exam while your stress is low and memory is sharp and clear. You also may want to ask your instructor if you can bring or use a blank piece of paper so you have more room to draw and write things out. Many of my students have found doing this alone increased their test scores.

❏ "THE ZONE"

Try not to come to class early on test day. Get to campus on time so you won't be late, but avoid the classroom until right before the test. You want to be on time, but you want to avoid talking with other students. This almost always ends with increased anxiety, and anxiety only impairs memory. Just as in sporting events, most professional athletes get into *the zone* before the event. You do not see them sitting or standing around talking with other athletes about the event. Why? Because they are getting into *the zone* and trying to relax. Again, if you have not properly studied, *it's too late*. However, it is not too late for damage control.

❏ DRESS FOR SUCCESS!

Make sure you dress appropriately. Now is not the time to be concerned with how you look but how you feel. Don't wear tight or restrictive clothing. It is always best to *dress in layers* so you have a control over your body temperature. It may be 105 degrees outside but only 68 degrees in your classroom. You need to be comfortable while taking the test, not distracted from being too hot or cold. Be sure what you are wearing is comfortable.

The greatest key to success in taking exams is the preparation done before the exam. The above are suggestions to help with a few common mistakes that students make, but they will do little to help if you have not properly prepared for the exam.

❑ MULTIPLE CHOICE TIPS/HINTS SHORT AND SWEET

- ✓ Cover all answers and answer in your head, then look for that answer from the options on the test.
- ✓ Answers to one question are frequently given away in another (thus the need for the speed suggestion).
- ✓ Answers with **absolutes** such as all, always, never, every, etc. are usually wrong.
- ✓ If two questions say the same thing, they are probably wrong unless there is "all the above" or "A & C" or something like that.
- ✓ If the answer has nothing to do with the question, even if it's true it's most likely wrong.
- ✓ If two answers are almost identical except for a few words, one of them is most likely the answer.
- ✓ Many would say that if you cannot make an educated guess and that out of four answers the third is the best guess. (I was not able to find significant research to back this but it would be my guess. I would definitely not choose the first.)
- ✓ **Never** argue with or add words to a question. Answer it **exactly** as it is written.
- ✓ Always eliminate wrong answers first if not sure of the correct answer.
- ✓ If there is no penalty for guessing, never leave a question blank!
- ✓ If you have no idea, some would say the longer answer is usually the correct answer. (With tips like this, I would

recommend using them as long as they prove to work. This means you will have to review your exams and take note of what worked and didn't work. I always make some sort of mark on my tests when I guess so I can evaluate such tips when reviewing the exam.)

✓ If there is a penalty for guessing, leave blank all questions that you don't know. (Consider answering if you can eliminate wrong answers or make a good educated guess.)

✓ If "All of the above" is an option and two answers are definitely correct, choose "All of the above."

✓ If "All of the above" is an option and one of the answers is definitely incorrect, do not choose "All of the above."

✓ Know your instructor. Try to get into their head and think, "How would they answer this question?"

✓ If there appears to be two answers and none of the choices allows for multiple answers, choose the **best** answer. This is actually in most directions: "Choose the best answer." Don't forget to consider what your *instructor* thinks the best answer is, not you.

✓ If one answer is totally different from the others, it is most likely incorrect. The remaining answers may be very similar, but only <u>one</u> of them is the correct answer.

✓ If three answers are saying the same thing, the different one is then correct. You can't have three right answers. Being similar is not the same as saying the same thing.

✓ Typically an answer that is extreme is incorrect. With problems solving questions such as math, chemistry, and physics, extreme answers are typically incorrect.

"However beautiful the strategy, you should occasionally look at the results" – Winston Churchill

THE ART
OF
MAKING
FLASH
CARDS

Flash cards can be one of the most effective methods of putting vast amounts of material to memory. The latest buzz word in educational circles is **application** rather than **memorization**. Coming from a long medical career and teaching medical professionals, I could not agree more with this concept. However, this debate has been frequently putting the cart before the horse. You cannot apply knowledge that you have not yet put to memory, at least not very effectively or efficiently. Though it is common sense, one of the biggest arguments against it is that technology provides instant access to whatever we want or need, 24/7. So **why** should you still have to memorize anything? The answer is so simple and obvious it seems ridiculous to even mention. Do you want your surgeon to have your anatomy memorized or need to reference a book or computer during surgery? What if you lose power? We still need to memorize things in school!

Another thing to mention: how you word your flash cards makes a big difference in the **memorization** versus **application** debate. You can word your flash cards to ask questions that include both. As you read more and get a chance to practice, you will see that flash cards can be so much more than just a simple memorization tool. There are far more applications and potential with flash cards than many give credit for. I see lots of arguments for such things as time lines, making charts, concept maps, note cards, etc., and I would argue that I could make more efficient flash cards for most every one of these, and in less time! I am not saying that there is no use for other tools in your learning tool box, but if done correctly, I think you will agree that flash cards are one of the best tools for certain subjects. For any subject that has lots of definitions, lists, tables, procedures, and items that you need to memorize, you can't beat flash cards.

The great advantage of using flash cards is that you are testing yourself as though you had your own personal tutor asking you questions. If you make flash cards **correctly**, you remove the question, "Do I really know the material?" You answer the question either correctly or incorrectly. You prepare yourself for exams much more effectively than by simply reading and reviewing notes. If you prepare your flash cards correctly, everything that is on the test will have been on your flash cards. Let's get started.

❏ FIRST THINGS FIRST

First of all, you have to read the book or take notes to make flash cards. You are going to use the material that you believe will be on the test to make your flash cards. The idea is to take **all** the information you want to memorize and be able to answer on a test, and put it on the flash cards. When you are done making the flash cards, you will be ready to study. This is the most critical part of making flash cards, because you do not want to make cards on material that will not be on the exam. It wastes your time! You either need to have great notes or you must have attended class to know what to use from the textbook.

❑ WHEN TO MAKE THEM....ASAP!!!

The best time to make flash cards is **right after** the material is presented in class and is fresh in your memory. This will prevent you from making cards on material that will not show up on the exam. The longer you wait to make your cards, the harder it will be to make them and the **more** time it will take (less time for fun).

Use your notes or the text as an outline for making your cards. When you are done, you should have all of your notes/text in question form on flash cards. **If done ASAP, this does not take long.** Sometimes I hear students say that it takes them too long to make their cards, and they don't think it's a good use of their time. However, that is because 99% of the time they have waited too long, and are often making other mistakes when creating their cards! When done correctly and as soon as possible, **flash cards do not take much time at all**. In fact, you can use this to help you determine if you are doing them correctly. Keep reading.

❑ ONLY WHAT YOU DON'T KNOW!!!!

You are only going to make flash cards on what you don't know. In other words, if you have something memorized, don't make a card on it even if it is going to be on the test. **It takes time**

to make the cards, and the idea is to be as efficient and effective with your time as possible. If you are not confident that you will remember some information, make a flash card on it. I can't stress this enough; this is the **number one mistake** I see students making. They make a flash card on **EVERYTHING**, and then say, "The flash cards don't work for me; they take too much time." When I ask them to bring some of their cards, I see they have everything on them including really simple stuff that they knew even before making the cards or taking the class. Why do they do this? It makes them feel better when they read their flash cards and know some of the answers. The problem is that it takes time. Time could be better spent on material that still needs to be memorized. Which is more important: feeling good while you study or getting the grade you want?

❏ YOUR PERSONAL TUTOR

You should ask a question on one side of the card and place the answer on the other side. Remember, you are creating your own personal tutor; you need to ask a question! This will allow you to test yourself and practice answering questions from memory. There is no question that you *know* the material if you can answer it from memory. This is very different than being able to recognize the correct answer.

Students have frequently come to see me after a test when they did not earn the grade they had hoped for and say, "I don't understand, I knew the material. I studied a lot and I was ready!" I say "Did you really study the appropriate amount of time, and were you ready to take the exam?" They always say "**YES.**" So I ask them a few simple recollection questions and they are unable to answer them or struggle to recall the information. Are they lying? Are they delusional? No, they really did study hard and they knew the material and understood it as they were **reading** and **reviewing** it. They truly thought they were prepared. When they were reading the terms, definitions, charts, and looking at diagrams, it all made perfect sense, but this **not** the same has having it memorized.

What they failed to do was to make sure that they had the necessary material **memorized** and that is where a study partner, practice tests, or flash cards can help. If someone asks you a question, you either know the answer or you don't. A study partner from your class is a great way to test your knowledge but it may be difficult to find times to get together more than once or twice. Practice tests are not going to have everything that is on your exam, and frequently contain many questions that are not.

Flash cards are the best method for practicing and testing what you have and have not memorized and the best thing about them is you can use them wherever and whenever you want. They are inexpensive and quick to make. If you make them correctly and can answer all of them before the exam, you know the material. No more "I **thought** I knew it."

Don't make the questions on your cards multiple choice or true/false. Just ask a **simple** question regarding a **small** piece of data. Your questions should be short answer, fill in the blank, list, name, identify, and describe. If you ask questions that are too long or complicated, you defeat the advantage of using a flash card. The military has a great saying: Keep It Simple, Stupid, or "KISS." Make **flash** cards (questions and answers), not **note** cards!

❏ WHAT WORDS TO USE

Use words like **list**, **define**, and **describe** in your questions. Flash cards are great for memorizing lists. Avoid open-ended or vague questions. This is not the place for essay questions. What would you want a tutor to ask you? Simple, straight, relevant questions that might appear on the exam. Think of multiple-choice questions without the choices. They are usually short and simple questions. If you can answer the multiple-choice questions without the choices, you are ready for the test!

Take your simple questions to a higher level that can include application whenever possible. If you have to list things, specify how to list them. For example: one of the sample flash cards asks you list the five layers of the epidermis. But it also asks you to do so from superficial (outer) to profundus (inner or deep). To answer this question you have to know both those words and typically you would then also visualize the answer. You have taken simple question and increased the level of comprehension and understanding. ***Do this whenever possible!***

❏ HOW MUCH IS TOO MUCH?

NOTE: Before you get started, it is fun to do an Internet search for the "definition of flash card" and read some of the results. You will repeatedly run across the words "briefly, brief, short, questions, answers, and quickly." Keep this in mind as you continue to read and as you make your cards later.

If a question requires a simple one- or two-word answer, you can ask several questions regarding the same topic on one card.

If you put more than one question on a card, number both the question and the answer. ***Do not put too much material on one flash card***. If you do is no longer a flash card and it has become a note card. Remember that the "flash" part is very important. "Flash" refers to quick and I have seen many cards that are not quick to read or answer. Premade "flash cards" are the perfect example. They are "text" or "note" cards, not flash cards.

If the question requires a lengthy or detailed answer, it is best to have just one question per card. Cards are not expensive, so try not to put too much material on one card. However, you do not want a stack of cards five inches thick for one exam. Remember, you want to be able to put these in your pocket so you can take them to work with you.

It is better to err on the side of too little rather than too much. The only real downside of too little is a *really thick* stack of flash cards. Look at all the sample below and you will see what I am talking about.

Your cards should be so short and simple that anyone can use them to ask you the questions without difficulty. Have a roommate, friend, or family member use your cards to quiz you.

❏ THIS IS NOT ENGLISH 101

You don't need to have full or proper sentences in your questions or answers. All you need is to ask and answer a question. **KEEP IT SIMPLE!** This is not something you will turn in so feel free to use abbreviations and symbols wherever and whenever possible. (See examples provided.) Remember, time is of the essence. The idea is to get your cards completed ASAP so you can spend more time using them.

❑ WHY THE 3X5 CARD?

It's best to use three-by-five note cards. They are small enough to easily fit in your pocket so you can take them to work, school, etc., and large enough to get the material you need on them. I have found that when students use larger cards they almost always start putting too much material on them. As soon as this happens they are no longer flash cards and have become note cards, and that is not what you want.

❑ KEEP THEM ORGANIZED

As you make your cards, develop some method for organizing them. If they are based on the chapters in a textbook, simply put the name or number of the chapter on the card. If they are based on your notes, you may want to organize them by subject. Either way, make sure you identify them so you can organize them later. You may also use colors for identification. Think about highlighting everything on one exam the same color. Then, for example, four exams would only require four different colored highlighters. (See the samples below.) This will allow you to quickly pull or add a chapter to a group of cards if you want to. If you don't do this, you will have to read every card to separate them for organization. This is very helpful when trading cards with friends and classmates and getting ready for exams, especially comprehensive exams.

❑ HOW TO USE YOUR CARDS

NOTE: *It is interesting to do an Internet search on "How to use flash cards" and see what comes up. There are various systems and algorithms available to describe how to use flash cards. It is my professional opinion they are making it entirely too complicated. Try my simple and easy to understand method and if that does not work for you, try some of the more "sophisticated and scientific" methods.*

Once you have your flash cards made, it is time to use them. You begin with all the flash cards in one stack for an exam. Start by reading the first card. Answer the question either in your head or out loud if this helps. Saying it out loud gives you the opportunity to practice pronunciation. After you have asked the question and answered it, then and **ONLY** then should you turn the card over to see if your answer was correct. If you answered it correctly and confidently (meaning you were certain of the answer, and didn't have to guess) put the card in a separate pile, called the "I got it" pile. If you answered the question incorrectly or were **not confident** in your answer, put the card at the back of your stack so you can try again later. If you had no idea what the answer is (this will happen a lot if you followed the directions, so don't panic), flip the card over and read the answer. Think about it, read the question and answer a few more times. Now flip the card over, ask the question again, and try to answer it. You can do this several times until you get the answer right, but you still have to put the card at the back of the pile. You only get to put the card in the "I got it" pile if you answer the card the first time correctly and with confidence.

Eventually you will have put all the cards in the "I got it" pile. This should happen one or two **DAYS** (not hours) before the exam.

Now you grab all the cards in the "I got it" pile (which should be all the cards at this point) and go through them again. You will find that you have forgotten some of the questions you got right or discover ones you were not confident with. This is normal, and this is why you gave yourself an extra day or two before the test so that you can **REVIEW**. This is what I was talking about in the Art of Studying when I said you should not "study" the day of the exam, only review.

I told you that you should only make cards on the material that you **don't** know. "I followed your directions, and yet I can answer so many of the cards the first time through. I didn't make cards on what I knew!" That's the beauty of it. By making the cards, you will remember approximately one-quarter to one-third of the material you are trying to learn. That's the whole point: to learn and remember.

Now that you have your cards made, you can easily take them to work or wherever you're going. Now you do not need an hour to study. You can pull your cards from your pocket at a fifteen-minute break (at work, home, school, etc.) and get through much of your stack. You should do this multiple times a day. **REPETITION** is the key!

❑ USING YOUR CARDS FOR REVIEW

It is important to remember that you only need small amounts of time to effectively study. Using your cards allows you to still have a life while in school. I have even used cards to study while watching my favorite TV program. This is essentially the same study method I described previously. Every commercial break, turn down the TV or hit mute and grab your cards. You will find that you can often get through the pile during the commercial breaks in a one-hour TV program.

Suppose you don't watch TV but you do have small children at home. Which is simpler: to find multiple five minute blocks of time when you could study using your cards, or to set aside a one one-hour block of uninterrupted time to use your notes or the text book to review?

You should review your cards throughout the day. Take fifteen or twenty minutes when you get up in the morning and run through your cards before going to work or school, at lunch break or between classes, and when you get home for the day. Do this again just before dinner and before going to bed. I found the most effective times for me were just before going to bed and first thing after waking up. Do the math – you will spend far less time doing this than "cramming," and you will be much more successful! This is what is called a win-win situation: less time studying with a better grade, less anxiety, and greater flexibility.

❏ "JEOPARDY"

After you have gone through all your cards and answered them correctly try taking a different approach to test your knowledge. Flip the entire stack over and read the answer side first as they do in the TV game show "Jeopardy." After reading the answer, state what the question should be. This is another way to stimulate your mind and help with retention and application. It is also a fun way to study with a group of classmates.

❑ SHARING CARDS

Flash cards are a great way to study with others and to keep on track. Take turns reading each other's cards to one another, or if you don't have time, try swapping cards for a day. By making flash cards and swapping them with other students, you can essentially study with others without actually finding a time that works for everyone. This can be extremely beneficial.

❑ SAVE YOUR MONEY!!

I recommend not using premade flash cards. Making your own cards is just as important as using them. Premade flash cards usually have way **too much** material to be called *flash* cards (remember the definitions you read on the internet?) and they often have material that you do not need to know for your exam. You will spend a great deal of time going through them to find what you do (or do not) need to know. You could have made your own cards in less time, saved a lot of money, and have done a better job. By making your own flash cards you are creating your own personal tutor, tailored just for you and your needs!

I call it "The Art of Making Flash Cards" for a reason. *It takes practice making flash cards* before you really get it down to an art. Once you figure out what method works best, you will wonder how you ever studied without them. Then, you have learned "The Art of Making Flash Cards."

KEY POINTS TO KEEP IN MIND:

SIMPLE - Keep them *simple* and short.

AVOID - *Avoid* too much information on one card.

ONLY - *Only* make cards on material that will be on the exam and that you do not currently know or remember.

FREQUENT - Short and *frequent* review of the cards is key.

NOTES - Use your class *notes* to make the cards.

I have provided sample flash cards from several different courses so you can see how you could use them for a variety of situations and courses.

SAMPLE FLASH CARDS:

Human Anatomy:

[question side] Chapter 2

1. name the 5 layers of the epidermis from superficial to profundus.

2. name the 2 layers of the dermis from superficial to profundus.

[Answer both questions in your head or out loud, then look at the answer.]

[answer side]

1. stratum corneum, lucidum, ganulosum, spinosum, and germinativum

2. papillary, reticular layer

[It should have taken only a minute or so to make this card.]

[question side] Chapter 5

1. name the 3 auditory ossicles from external to internal.

2. where are they found?

[Remember, don't worry about sentence structure; "simple."]

[answer side]

1. malleus, incus, stapes

2. middle ear

Physiology:

[question side] The Cell

1. function of smooth ER? [Abbreviate ER; you are studying for the test, and you know what ER stands for. If not, make a flash card for it.]

2. function of rough ER?

3. function of golgi apparatus?

[answer side]

1. synthesis of lipids, hormones, and glycogen

2. covered with ribosomes and primarily responsible for protein synthesis and packaging

3. modifies and packages secretions

[question side] Muscle

1. what is a single contractile unit of muscle called?

2. what is the cell membrane of a muscle cell called?

3. where is calcium stored in the muscle cell?

[answer side]

1. sarcomere

2. sarcolemma

3. sarcoplasmic reticulum

Pharmacology:

[question side] Chapter 1

1. list the 4 components of pharmacokinetics.

2. define pharmacokinetics.

[answer side]

1. absorption, distribution, metabolism, elimination

2. how the body affects the drug

[question side] Drugs for hypertension

Beta Blockers

1. Therapeutic class (TC): *[when making flash cards, use abbreviations when ever possible to save time!]* Pharmacological class (PC):

2. Action (A):

3. Side effects (SE): (fatigue, weakness, depression), impotence, hypotension

---

[answer side]

1. TC: antiarrhythmic and antihypertensive
   PC: beta blocker

2. A: blocks effects of catecholamines on $beta_1$ receptor sites

3. SE: BRADYCARDIA (fatigue, weakness, depression), impotence, hypotension

Pathophysiology:

[question side] Pulmonary system

Chronic Bronchitis

1. what is it?

2. cause?

3. manifestations?

4. evaluation and Treatment?

[answer side]

1. chronic inflammation of bronchi defined by mucous gland hyperplasia, muscle hypertrophy, and bronchial wall thickening.

2. chronic exposure to irritants and/or infection

3. increased mucus production, increased size and number of glands, mucus produced is thick, ciliary function is impaired, increased susceptibility to pulmonary infections. SOB & wheezing

4. PFT, ABGs, and CXR with history. Tx – bronchodilators and expectorants.

[question side] Renal system

Acute pyelonephritis

1. what is it?

2. cause?

3. manifestations?

4. evaluation and Treatment?

[answer side]

1. infection of the renal pelvis

2. most often caused by urinary obstruction and reflux along with bacteria (E. coli). Untreated UTIs

3. flank or back PAIN, fever, frequency, dysuria

4. UA and history, treated with antibiotics

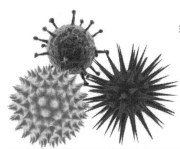

Biology:

[question side] Chapter 2

1. the structural and functional unit of all living things?

2. name the 2 methods of transport across a membrane.

3. movement of substances from high to low?

[answer side]

1. the cell

2. active and passive transport

3. diffusion

[question side] Chapter 11

1. division of the cell that creates identical cells with 46 chromosomes?

2. division of a cell that results in 2 cells with 23 chromosomes?

[answer side]

1. mitosis

2. meiosis

Psychology:

[question side]

1. name Freud's 5 psychosexual stages in order and period of life (ages)

[answer side]

1. first year of life: Oral stage
2. ages 1-3: Anal stage
3. ages 3-6: Phallic stage
4. ages 6-12: Latency stage
5. ages 12-18: Genital stage

[question side]

1. define psychology.

2. who was the "father" of the psychodynamic perspective?

3. who was the "father" of the behavioral perspective?

[answer side]

1. scientific study of behavior and mental processes

2. Sigmund Freud

3. John B. Watson

Chemistry:

[question side]

1. elements that carry an electrical charge are called?

2. elements with a positive charge are called?

3. elements with a negative charge are called?

[answer side]

1. ions

2. cation

3. anion

[question side]

1. a chemical bond caused by transferring of electrons?

2. a chemical bond caused by sharing of electrons?

[answer side]

1. ionic bond

2. covalent bond

SCIENCE LABS

Science labs are ***very different*** from science lectures. Class is usually lecture based, whereas labs are hands-on with a lot of activity and interaction. Labs such as chemistry, physiology, biology, and physics are very organized and much of the lab is planned out before the course begins. The best approach to these types of labs is proper preparation. You will have a certain amount of work to accomplish in a given amount of time. The more prepared you are the smoother and quicker the lab will go. (Not all of the suggestions below will apply to every lab.)

Anatomy labs usually involve more independent study in which the student has a great deal of control over their activities and time. This actually is the most difficult type of lab for students because they are completely responsible for what they do with their lab time. If done correctly, this can be the most beneficial format for learning. If done incorrectly, it is the worst and most challenging format for a student to learn.

The following is a checklist for science labs. Use this list to see what you have and have not tried. Use it to come up with a game plan if needed. Not all suggestions will apply to every kind of lab.

❑ PREVIOUS SUGGESTIONS

Many of the previous suggestions also apply to lab, so be sure to read them first.

❑ LAB PREPARATION

Before attending any lab, you will want to do some reading. You should actually read **all** the exercises and activities that you will perform that day. For lecture I told you not to read but skim; it is the complete opposite here. You will want to read and take notes *before* coming to lab. For labs involving experiments, you will want to be very familiar with what you are going to be doing. You may even want to highlight some important things to remember that you would not want to forget or miss.

Flag or mark the pages in your text that you may need to reference while you work. It is difficult to get through an anatomy lab without the use of a text with pictures and diagrams. Flag all of the pages that have the pictures of the structures you are going to look at during that lab. Highlight all the structures on the diagram in the text that have been indicated in your lab manual or notes. Highlight not just the name of the structure, but also some of the line going to the actual structure on the picture. As I mentioned recommended earlier in the Art of Studying, when you cover the names with a note card or your hand, you are able to tell what lines needed to be identified.

❑ MAKING THE MOST OF LAB

Most labs are several hours long. There is usually a lot of self-study or independent time for the students, and it is very easy to lose motivation and focus. You have taken several hours out of your life to be in class. For many it is time away from work or family. Use this time carefully. You will not have the supplies (models,  cadavers, microscopes, experiments, etc.) at home that are available in the lab. You will spend two to three times longer trying to learn just from a book than what you can do in lab. Take as many breaks as you need in order to stay focused and sharp. Avoid the temptation to leave early if your instructor allows you to. You will have to spend more time studying at home than you would if you had just stayed in lab and remained focused. If you use lab time efficiently, you may have to only review at home before the lab exams instead of studying for hours. The key to using lab time to its fullest is to *stay busy*. All of the following suggestions will help you use your time wisely.

❑ CHOOSING YOUR LAB PARTNER(S)

Choose your lab partner(s) carefully! This can be just as critical as how much you study and prepare. The right partner can lift you up and greatly increase your performance. The wrong partner can take you down in flames. You will want to surround yourself with motivated individuals. Motivation is contagious. We all have days of low energy and motivation. However, if we are with a group of students who are focused and motivated, their energy usually rubs off on us and increases our productivity. If you find yourself sitting at a table with students who don't want to be there, are nonproductive, or complain a lot, then *move!* If seating is assigned, ask to be reassigned. Motivation is contagious, but so are discontent, negativity, and lack of motivation. If you feel uncomfortable changing partners or tables, ask yourself what is more important to you: what others in the lab might think about you, or your grade?

"Tis better to be alone, than in bad company" – George Washington

❑ PREPARING FOR LAB EXAMS

The best way to prepare for lab exams is to use lab time to the fullest. The more productive you were during the lab the week before, the better you will do on the exam. You really cannot make up lab time at home. Outside of the lab, the best way to prepare is to review what was done in lab. Many lab quizzes will be much similar to lecture exams in both preparation and execution.

Anatomy labs will be very different. Using visuals such as diagrams from your textbook and computer images, and attending open lab sessions will be the most helpful. Most instructors will not have a problem with students taking pictures of the models to look at when they get home. It is almost always **unacceptable** to take pictures of human cadavers. Believe it or not, I have had a number of students doing this with their smart phones.

Another thing that many of my students have found very helpful is the Internet. Find sites that have visual quizzes set up. Many of the quizzes will actually use the same models you used in your lab. They are worth looking at. Do a simple Internet search and you will find dozens of free opportunities. Just remember that the best way to prepare for a visual exam is to study visually.

❑ "TAKE A BREAK"

Science labs can feel very long! It is easy to lose focus and get tired. Especially when they occur at the end of the day and you have already had a full day of work, school, studying, or activities. Take several breaks if possible. Even just walking to the drinking fountain can be enough to refresh you. You will actually waste more time sitting around tired and unmotivated than you would if you took several short breaks. To make the most of your lab time you must be alert and focused. As stated before, most labs cannot be made up; this is your one chance, so make the most of it.

❏ HUMAN ANATOMY LAB ACTIVITIES

College anatomy labs are often independent, allowing the student to study whatever he or she needs at their own pace. This can be *very* independent, putting the responsibility on the student to cover the material. Anatomy lab is frequently different from other labs that have specific experiments set up, along with a list of tasks that must be accomplished in a specified amount of time. This structure keeps students on track, motivated, and focused. If your anatomy lab is independent study and lacks this structure, create your own structure with activities. The following is a list of suggestions to help keep you focused.

BREAK IT DOWN:

Break down the lab into smaller, more manageable tasks. Figure out how much time you have in lab to actually study, and then divide that time by how many tasks you have created. Keep to your time schedule so that you do not fall behind.

For example, if you are to study muscles that day, break it down into four or five tasks. The first task is study just the muscles of the head, face, and neck. This would all be on the typical "head" model. The second task is to go through the shoulder and arm muscles. This task also correlates well with a typical lab model of the arm and shoulder region. Next would be muscles of the torso, and finally the leg.

When you are figuring how much time to allot for each task, always add in a little extra time. Inevitably, it takes a little longer than originally planned. If you get through the tasks faster than you planned, then you will have time at the end to go back and review any area needing additional study. Before you know it, you are out of time and lab is over. I typically assigned these tasks to my anatomy lab students and gave them their time deadlines based on experience, but you many have a passive instructor and will need to do this yourself.

QUIZ, QUIZ, QUIZ:

After you have completed each task, run back through each lab model and quiz your lab partner. Better yet, quiz the whole table. If you are fortunate enough to have a cadaver, you can apply the same concept. Any time you find yourself bored or you have "nothing" to do (which should *never* happen in any science lab), quiz a classmate or ask to be quizzed. Quizzing keeps you engaged and greatly enhances memory retention.

CHECK OFF:

After you complete each task and have reviewed the material a few times, have your lab instructor watch you as you identify all of the assigned structures. If you name the structures out loud, the instructor can correct your pronunciation, if needed. Do this for each task to make sure you are identifying and pronouncing everything correctly. You will find this helps break up the material, keeps you focused, and makes the time go by quickly.

END-OF-CLASS REVIEW:

There are several things you can do to review at the end of lab, but you will most likely need permission and help from your instructor. Ask for his or her help in doing some of these activities. Here are two examples:

TEAM ANATOMY-DRAWING GAME

Divide the class into two teams. Each team will need a piece of paper. As a team, write down ten to twenty of the structures that were covered in that lab and number them. This should take about five minutes. Each team will need a volunteer to draw the other team's list on the board. This is a team anatomy-drawing game, and the rules are as follows:

1. You will have two to five minutes to complete the list. You want to make it difficult to complete them all in the allotted time so there is a sense of urgency; this adds to the fun.
2. One person from each team will draw the entire list.
3. The list MUST be drawn in order as numbered on the paper.
4. If you get stuck or do not know what the item is, you may "pass" or skip it. However, every item passed is a point for the other team.
5. You may draw anything you like to get your team to say the correct word, but you may NOT speak.
6. As you draw the structures, your team shouts out the answers. When you hear the correct answer, shout back the correct answer so EVERYONE can hear and knows the correct answer. Don't forget this! This is the most important part because everyone needs to know what you were drawing and what the correct answer was. The instructor plays referee and WILL need to remind the students of this.
7. The team guessing CANNOT simply shout out all the terms covered. The answers need to be logical and honest attempts. If the team just starts shouting out all terms covered, the referee (instructor) passes that term and the other team gets the point.

8. The person drawing may take materials along to help him or her draw. They get no more than one minute to review the list and ask the instructor questions before beginning.

NOTE: *Feel free to change the rules in any way. If you do more than one lab exercise per lab, simply combine them all for this activity. This is just one example of how to do a fun review. If you have another lab next door, you may even want to challenge them to a game, lab versus lab. You may want to reward the winning team with getting to leave lab first or having the losing team clean up. Mix it up and individualize as you see fit. My students loved this review.* **Have fun!**

ANATOMY MANIA

Each table (team) generates a list of twenty (or whatever number is determined) numbered items covered in that day's lab session on a piece of paper. The items must be able to be seen on the provided models. For example, if you covered the skull, your list might look like this:

1. Squamosal suture
2. Crista galli
3. Mandibular arch
4. Mastoid process
5. Mental foramen

Take up to five minutes to complete your list. Pick the twenty most difficult items you can think of, or the items that you think you would most likely miss on a quiz. One designated person from each table will go to another table with his or her table's list. All of the tables do this at the same time. Each designated person or quizzer will have two minutes to read his or her list to another table of students. The list must be read in order. **Everyone** at the table must point to the correct term on the model before moving on to the next item. If they do not know the structure, they can pass and move to the next item in order. The team that made the list gets the point for any passed items; they cannot come back to them. The instructor plays referee, starts and stops each session, and keeps track of each team's points on the board. When the two minutes has ended, the quizzer will tell the instructor how many points (one point for each item) the team got and how many were passed. The instructor will then say, "Switch," and each quizzer moves to another table. You repeat this until the quizzer gets back to his or her own table. At this point, you can either have the quizzer quiz his or her own table or have the table take the list and quiz the quizzer. I usually drop the time by half for this because they have just had several reviews of the list and should be able to complete the list in less time. Try to pick a time limit that is challenging for completing the list. It adds a little stress and intensity (fun). You should see the scores go up as the game progresses. Hint: each table might want to use just one model in the center of the table. Those who are having difficulty identifying can benefit from those who know the material better. This activity works for the majority of anatomy labs and is a great learning tool.

HEALTHCARE LABS

Healthcare labs are very similar to science labs in many ways and most every suggestion above can be applied to them as well. After teaching nursing students for many years, the one thing I observed causing students the most problems when they needed to be checked off in lab by one of their instructors was their nerves. Students are their own worst enemy in labs and clinicals. Most were prepared and could perform the tasks satisfactorily if the instructor was not observing them. Their anxiety caused them to forget things and make simple mistakes.

There are two ways to better prepare for these kinds of lab activities. The first is practice enough so that even under stress you respond from muscle memory. This may take a lot of practice if you really get nervous from having an instructor observe and grade your performance.

The other method was already mentioned on page 42 "Practice Performing Under Stress And Time." Apply the same concept here. The key is to get comfortable with performing under stress and being observed. You will not be alone; many of your classmates will have this same issue. Identify them and form a study or practice group. The more students, the better! You want to perform in front of as many different people as possible. Try to have a different lab partner every time you practice, and also have your partner try to intimidate and distract you. It may sound a little strange, but you perform how you practice. Be sure to have them time you, and if you only get 30 minutes in class to perform, practice doing it in 20 or 25 minutes. This actually can be a lot of fun for students and builds confidence. You will be amazed how much better you perform in front of instructors by practicing this way.

Another really fun activity is to have teams in the skills lab. Have everyone perform the same skill and do time trials. The person that does the skill the quickest and with the least mistakes wins. Have several teams perform at the same time right next to each other. This will really get the adrenaline going, it's fun, and builds confidence and skills. By doing this, you will also get to observe others doing it and maybe get ideas of different or better ways of doing it. You also get to grade, judge, and observe other students, which greatly contributes to your learning of the skill.

Example: Most health care professions have to be able to put on sterile gloves while maintaining the sterility of the gloves. Have one to four students with a sterile glove package ready to go. The timekeeper says, "**GO**" and starts the time. Other students that will be competing can taunt them and try to distract them. Everyone else watches for breaks in sterility. You make up your own rules just as long as it's consistent. You can keep using the same pair of gloves if supplies are limited (as they usually are) and just put them back as best you can for the next person. We had a lot of fun in lab with this one!

You could do this same type of exercise for studying to be an EMT, paramedic, respiratory therapist, medical doctor, physician assistant, nurse practitioner, surgical technician, or any military healthcare provider. The military uses this type of training all the time for other activities; why not use this technique for healthcare profession students?

If you only practice with the same person in ideal circumstances with no time limit, you should not be perplexed as to why you get nervous when testing in front of your instructor. You can apply this activity to drawing up medication(s) (be careful with needles), putting in urinary catheters, dressing changes, physical assessments, neurological checks, bed changes, giving medications, BLS, etc. The best part of all is that this really helps, it's a blast, it makes practicing fun, and the time flies. Try it – what do you have to lose?

CONCLUSION!

"Education is the most powerful weapon which you can use to change the world" – Nelson Mandela

Congratulations! You have made one the greatest, maybe the most important, choices of your life: your education. Your education is the greatest gift you can give to yourself. It must be *earned*; it cannot be given to you by someone else. It will not be easy. If it were, everyone would have one. Fact is, it's quite difficult at times and frequently costs a great deal of money. What is so great about an education? Well, name something else that you earn that can never, *never* be taken away from you. You can lose your car, your house, or your money—you can even lose your life—but no one can ever take your education from you. Education cannot and should not be easy. It would have no value if it *were* easy.

With that said, you don't want to make it any more difficult than it already is. How you study is the most important key to your educational success. How you show up for class is just as critical. Make sure you are prepared to do what is necessary in order to be successful in your education. If you're not prepared to make some sacrifices, I would recommend waiting until you are. Your education costs too much money not to take it seriously. I have given you a lot to think about and implement. The most important thing to remember is that studying really is an art. It has to be learned, practiced, and molded into something unique for you. It really is simple in concept. If you are getting the grades you want, then you must have figured it out, so simply keep doing what you're doing. If you are not getting the grades you want, then something is missing and/or needs to be changed. I have given you pages of ideas and suggestions to help you formulate a plan of action or a new game plan should things change. It is well worth your time to figure it out sooner rather than later. Your very future and career could depend on it!

"Stupidity is also a gift of God, but one mustn't misuse it" – Pope John Paul II

One could say stupidity is doing the exact same thing over and over and expecting a different result. With that being said, if you are not doing well in class, do **NOT** keep doing the same things and expect a different result. You may need to review this book *several* times to figure out what works best for you. You may want to consider taking notes or even highlighting as you read it a second or third time. You have all the tools you need to be successful in school. All that is left is doing the work. I wish you the best of luck in your educational journey.

Sincerely,

Drew

.